T0375275

SPORTS CONCUSSION AND NECK TRAUMA

PREVENTING INJURY FOR FUTURE GENERATIONS

Dr. Kelly J. Roush,
Certified Chiropractic Sports Physician,
Certified Athletic Trainer

authorHOUSE®

AuthorHouse™
1663 Liberty Drive
Bloomington, IN 47403
www.authorhouse.com
Phone: 1-800-839-8640

Published by AuthorHouse 2/6/2012

ISBN: 978-1-4685-2572-4 (sc)
ISBN: 978-1-4685-2571-7 (hc)
ISBN: 978-1-4685-2570-0 (e)

Library of Congress Control Number: 2011963468

CONTENTS

ACKNOWLEDGMENTS

I would first and foremost like to thank God for giving me the opportunity to serve these athletes and the opportunity to make a difference each and every day. I would sincerely like to thank my husband, Allen and our two beautiful children, Jared and Grace for giving me the time to put this book together and for supporting me through this endeavor. For my staff's assistance with computer assistance and support, I offer a hearty thanks. I would like to thank Holland Photography and Eric Roberts (athlete in pictures in chapter 5), and a big thank-you to those who provided interviews for the book: Carol Shank; MJ, Larry, and Rhonda Russell; Rodney Zide, president of Zides Sports Shop and of Proline, Inc.; former NFL player Mike Bartrum; and Dr. Bill Moreau. I would like to thank the trainers and team physicians I have worked with over the years for their dedication and for encouraging me to get this book to the public. I would also like to thank Author House for their guidance and assistance in publishing this book.

INTRODUCTION

This text includes a discussion of the definition, types of injury, grades of injury, assessment, treatment, return-to-play decisions, equipment considerations, and actual case scenarios of head and neck trauma in athletics. It also includes an example of an emergency medical plan, sample evaluation tools, and review of the most current research. This text was written with the main goal of educating athletes, coaches, and parents of athletes but may be utilized as an educational component for sports medicine professionals. This book focuses primarily on football injuries due to the prevalence of head/neck injury in football but may apply to any sport.

Statistics reveal that over three hundred thousand sports-related concussions occur annually. One out of five high school American football players suffer a concussion annually. The risk of sustaining a concussion in football is four to six times greater for a player who has sustained a previous concussion. In football, the majority of injuries to the head result from making a tackle (43 percent), being tackled (23 percent), blocking (20 percent), or being blocked (10 percent). Although it is estimated that a third of sports-related head injuries are due to football; gymnastics, boxing, wrestling, hockey, soccer, pole vaulting, bobsledding, skiing, baseball, softball, volleyball, and basketball are other sports in which concussion is prevalent.

Sooner or later, every coach, parent, and sports professional faces the difficult task of determining whether the athlete has sustained a concussion and when he or she can return to play. Subjective information (questioning the athlete) is not enough. Athletes typically will downplay their injury in an attempt to continue playing, and it is difficult to explain to an athlete who "appears" to be fine why he or she can't go back in the game.

It is my goal to help reduce the incidence of head- and neck-related trauma in athletics. This book provides education on specific clinical history to look for during the pre-sports physical exam; provides objective tools to help providers make better return-to-play decisions; and educates athletes, coaches, and parents on the danger of continuing to play with a probable head/neck injury and how to do their part to prevent further injury. This book includes personal interviews including the mother of a football player who collapsed after a game while walking to the locker room and died of a head injury; a dad whose fifteen-year-old, 6'1", 220-pound son was simply riding his bicycle without a helmet on when he wrecked and suffered several facial fractures and a serious head injury; and an interview with the US Olympic Committee Director of Sports Medicine, Dr. Bill Moreau, who also has earned his diplomat as a Sports Chiropractic Physician. This book includes an interview with Rodney Zide, CEO of Zides Sport Shop and Proline, Inc. whom is one of the leaders in the football helmet reconditioning and equipment fitting industry and an interview with Mike Bartrum, a former NFL football player, who sustained a cervical disk injury.

In this book, I also share my own evaluation tools and return-to-play guidelines. I share case scenarios from personal experiences of dealing with head/neck trauma as a certified chiropractic sports physician and certified athletic trainer.

Preventing Injury for Future Generations

PREFACE

It was a beautiful fall evening, not too hot, not too cold. The leaves were in full color in southeast Ohio, and there was a slight breeze. I remember telling the certified athletic trainer as we walked across the field to the sideline, "It's a perfect night for football," as we listened to the band play and teams chant while they performed their warm-up routine. Although it may seem odd for a woman, I absolutely love football. I had received my bachelor's degree in sports medicine/athletic training at the University of Charleston and had just completed an additional five-year academic program at Palmer College of Chiropractic, which included an extensive component of neuromuscular education. My ultimate goal has always been to be a team physician. While at Palmer, I trained and traveled with Olympic potential pole vaulters, trained Olympic bobsledders, provided sports injury coverage for a semipro hockey team, worked with our nationally ranked rugby team, and worked as an athletic trainer at both college and NFL football camps during my summer breaks. I received a great deal of hands-on experience in evaluating and managing head and neck trauma.

On that particular night, I simply rode to the game with the trainer who was asked to cover the game for the team's usual grad student trainer. Neither of us knew the players or the coaches of this team, and we certainly weren't aware that the events of that night would change our lives forever.

It was a close game, with a score of 21–20. As the winning team headed to the locker room to celebrate, one of their players collapsed on the pavement. One of the assistant coaches came and told me the trainer needed me; there was "a kid sick." I ran toward the locker room and found the athlete—Matt—kneeling on the pavement, holding his head in his hands. I asked him what his name was, and he mumbled it. I asked what was wrong, and he mumbled, "My head is killing me." He then looked up at me, and his green eyes literally seemed to explode in front of me.

Matt had an aneurysm, which means a main blood vessel in his brain had ruptured. He had a brain hemmorhage. His pupils were fixed, and his vitals were erratic. We immediately cut his pads away from his chest, got oxygen to him, and provided emergency procedures. EMS had already left the field. Only by the Grace of God were we able to keep him alive long enough for him to be flown to a trauma center, but the damage to his brain was irreversible. He was taken off life support the next day.

After the funeral, I learned a lot more about Matt's history. His mom told me he had taken a hard hit to the head several weeks prior to that night, a hit several fans and coaches remembered as well. Experts watched a video of that game, and there was no evidence of any particular hit that would likely have caused this significant head trauma. His autopsy report determined Matt's death was the result of swelling on the brain caused by a brain hemorrhage. The autopsy report stated, "It is probable that the hemorrhage was caused by a direct blow to the head   It's possible that this injury occurred while playing football." Matt had shown signs of being excessively tired during the two weeks prior to the fatal event. After his death. fellow athletes told us he had headaches, but they had not relayed this information to the school trainer, his parents, or coaches.

Matt loved football and took and delivered some hard hits. After reviewing his history, I am quite convinced that he died from second-impact syndrome, which means he had taken a blow to the head probably two weeks prior, continued playing, and took more minor hits that caused additional swelling and pressure on his brain. Finally, the vessels of the brain ruptured.

I had nightmares after that event. I would wake up looking at his eyes, which just seemed to explode in front of me. And I was mad at God. How could he take this young athlete, and why was I there? I wasn't supposed to be there. I had nothing to do with that team at the time, and I had just spent a decade training to help prevent this type of injury. I had been interested in head and neck trauma prior to Matt's injury, but since his death, I have been driven to find out why this happened. I want to do everything in my power to prevent it from happening to someone else. At the funeral, the minister made the comment, "God does not make mistakes. It's hard for you and I to see the purpose, and it's definitely hard to accept it."

Matt had put his faith in Jesus Christ, when two men from a church talked with him the day before the game in which he collapsed and died. God put me at that game for a reason, and maybe it was to write this book and to prompt me to educate others about concussion and neck trauma and the long-term effects that can be associated with that trauma.

About six months after his death, I had a dream. There was a bright light and a voice that was so clear. It said, "Do what you're meant to do." It was so real that I woke up shaking. But at that moment, I was overcome by the most peaceful feeling, and the nightmares stopped.

Prior to that event, I had spent ten years of my life studying and preparing myself to become a team physician, and I had assessed hundreds of concussions. After going through that horrible ordeal with the team, the community, the family, and the coaches, they asked me to be their team physician. This school, like many rural high schools, had no team doctor to watch over their kids, and I served as their team physician for thirteen years. I obtained a postgraduate specialty as a Certified Chiropractic Sports Physician, and I have read tons of articles, watched numerous programs on head trauma, and even observed brain surgery, looking for the answer as to how this athlete could be smiling and celebrating with teammates just minutes before collapsing into a comatose state. I currently speak locally and nationally about concussion and neck trauma. I have written newspaper articles, taught coaches' clinics and sessions at sports medicine conferences, and I train other team physicians (MD, DO, DC) how to provide emergency care and on field assessment of the athlete. I developed the sports medicine program at the multidisciplinary clinic, where I work and currently serve as the director of sports medicine services. We provide twenty local high schools with financial stipends to provide athletic training services; we provide fourteen of those schools with team physicians. Our goal is to make every attempt to keep these athletes safe. I assist with helmet fitting and make return-to-play decisions for concussed athletes. I have had this internal drive to write and publish this book to prevent this type of catastrophic injury from ever occurring again.

My passion is head and neck trauma.
My mission is to prevent injury for future generations.

DEDICATION

This book is dedicated to Matt Ault, a young football player who died of second-impact syndrome; to all the other athletes who have sustained life-changing or catastrophic injury; to The Zides family, who have dedicated fifty-three years to preventing head trauma by teaching proper fitting of equipment and designing safer equipment; and to all of the athletic trainers and team physicians who work endless hours to keep these athletes safe.

CHAPTER 1

DEFINITION OF HEAD INJURY/WHAT IS A CONCUSSION? TYPES OF HEAD INJURY/WHAT IS SECOND-IMPACT SYNDROME?

There are various types of injuries to the head, with the most common being a concussion or traumatic brain injury, sometimes referred to as a TBI. A traumatic brain injury is defined as a blow or jolt to the head or related structure that disrupts the normal function of the brain.

Depending on the extent of damage to the brain, symptoms of a traumatic brain injury may be mild, moderate, or severe. Mild cases may result in a brief change in mental state or consciousness, while severe cases may result in extended periods of unconsciousness, coma, or even death. Loss of consciousness is not required for an injury to be a concussion. The distinction between the degrees of concussion is based on signs and symptoms. Signs/symptoms of a concussion can show up right away or may take days or weeks to appear. Following is a list of the most common signs/symptoms of a sports-related concussion:

PHYSICAL SIGNS/SYMPTOMS OF A CONCUSSION

HEADACHE * DIZZINESS * NAUSEA * SENSITIVITY TO
LIGHT * BALANCE PROBLEMS

VISUAL PROBLEMS * VOMITING * CONFUSION * SLURRED SPEECH
SENSITIVITY TO NOISE * FATIGUE * NUMBNESS/TINGLING OF HEAD, FACE, OR HANDS

COGNITIVE SIGNS/SYMPTOMS OF CONCUSSION

HAS DIFFICULTY CONCENTRATING * REPEATS QUESTIONS * ANSWERS QUESTIONS SLOWLY
FEELS MENTALLY IN A FOG * HAS DIFFICULTY REMEMBERING * IS CONFUSED ABOUT EVENTS
IS FORGETFUL OF RECENT INFORMATION

EMOTIONAL SIGNS/SYMPTOMS OF CONCUSSION

IRRITABILITY * SADNESS * EXCESSIVE DISPLAYS OF EMOTION * NERVOUSNESS

SLEEP-RELATED SIGNS/SYMPTOMS OF CONCUSSION

DROWSINESS * SLEEPING LESS THAN NORMAL * SLEEPING MORE THAN NORMAL * TROUBLE FALLING ASLEEP
("Concussion Facts")

Coaches may notice the athlete appears dazed or is confused about an assignment, particular plays, or position on the field. The athlete may appear to be clumsy, answer questions slowly, and/or show behavioral or personality changes. The athlete may not be able to recall events prior to or after the hit or specific tackling event. The athlete may argue or laugh excessively. Coaches and other team members should observe any behavior that is not normal for the athlete and report it to the medical professional— such as the licensed athletic trainer or team physician—immediately.

When a football player takes a hit to the head, the force of that blow averages ninety-eight times the force of gravity. Most hits occur from a blow to the side of the head, often on the lower half of the face. The pressure from the hit passes through the brain and bounces off the skull.

The concussion occurs on the opposite side of the brain (contre coupe injury; "School of Hard Knocks").

Sports-related trauma causes many types of head injuries. A common complication of a blow to the head is cerebral contusion, causing increased intracranial pressure in the skull due to an increase of cerebrospinal fluid and/or occurrence of an intracranial bleed. Computer tomography (CT) is commonly used to detect this type of injury, and surgical decompression is typically performed if herniation is present.

Hematomas, localized swelling filled with blood resulting from a break in a blood vessel, in the intracranial cavity are categorized by three anatomical locations.

1. Subdural Hematoma: A subdural hematoma is the most fatal athletic head injury and occurs between the dural surface and the leptomeninges covering the brain. These hematomas are venous in nature and are often associated with contusion of the white matter of the brain. Acute subdural hematomas result from bleeding within the subdural space as a result of stretching and tearing of subdural veins. Athletes with an acute subdural hematoma may be alert and awake, neurological deficits may not show up immediately and could take up to a three-week duration to appear). However, the majority of athletes with any sizable acute subdural hematoma present with an altered state of consciousness, major neurological deficits, and coma. Athletes with an acute subdural hematoma are often unconscious and sustain diffuse, irreversible brain damage ("Subdural Hematoma").

Symptoms of a subdural hemorrhage/hematoma have a slower onset than those of an epidural hemorrhage because veins bleed slower than arteries as a result of their lower pressure. Signs/symptoms of a subdural hematoma may show up within twenty-four hours but may be delayed as much as two weeks. Subdural hematomas occur around the top and side of the frontal and parietal lobes. They also occur in the posterior cranial fossa and near the falx cerebri and tentorium cerebelli. Athletes on blood thinners, taking aspirin, or drinking alcohol are more susceptible to a subdural hematoma and may develop a bleed from even a minor head injury.

A chronic subdural hematoma is rare but can be dangerous (over three-week duration). This type of hematoma results in a small amount of bleeding that becomes surrounded by a semipermeable membrane. This membrane then attracts tissue fluid through osmotic pressure. The fluid passes through the membrane, which increases the size of the hematoma. This process may continue for several months as the brain gradually adapts to the increasing pressure. A chronic subdural hematoma is defined as a hematoma present three weeks or more after a traumatic injury (Bailes and Hudson). The athlete may present with clinical symptoms, such as mental disturbance, personality changes, focal transient neurologic deficits, nuchal rigidity, photophobia (sensitivity to light), or a slow progression of neurological signs of severe and progressive headache (Robinson). A CT scan is commonly performed to detect subdural hematoma, which typically reveals a concave appearance. Treatment may include monitoring with CT imaging, anti-epileptic medication, and, if mass effect or neurologic deficits, surgical evacuation.

2. EPIDURAL HEMATOMA: An epidural hematoma is located between the dura and the skull and is caused by a rupture of the middle meningeal artery, commonly caused by a linear fracture of the temporal bone. Most epidural hematomas are associated with a skull fracture that leads to a laceration of the middle meningeal artery or vein. Epidural hematomas are typically characteristic of an isolated injury to the skull, dura, and dural vessels. The athlete may clinically present with a lucid interval. The athlete will lose consciousness and then appear asymptomatic and may have a normal neurological exam. However, the injury to the skull or vessels leads to a slow accumulation of blood in the epidural space, compressing the brain stem and causing a rapid progression toward neurologic dysfunction, brain hemorrhage, and possibly death (Bailes and Hudson).

SYMPTOMS OF A SKULL FRACTURE

*LEAKAGE OF CSF FLUID FROM THE NOSE, MOUTH, OR EAR (clear, sweet fluid)
*VISIBLE DEFORMITY OR DEPRESSION OF HEAD OR FACE
*AN EYE THAT CANNOT MOVE OR IS DEVIATED TO ONE SIDE
*BRUISING OF THE EYES OR FACE

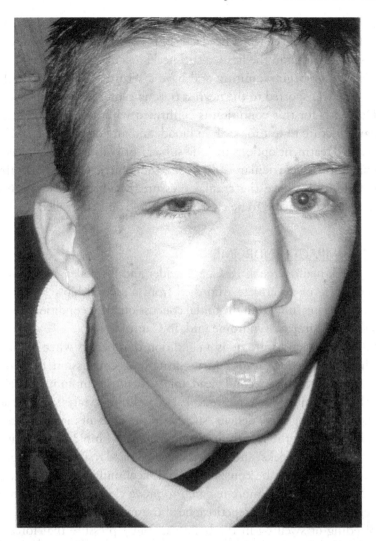

3. SUBARACHNOID HEMORRHAGE: A
subarachnoid hemorrhage is an abnormal dilation of an artery that causes vasospasm and, most often, a stroke. This may occur in athletics yet be completely unrelated to head trauma—possibly caused by a congenital aneurysm. It may also occur in conjunction with diffuse cerebral damage resulting from a serious head trauma caused by impact. A subarachnoid hemorrhage is a common cause of sudden death in young people.

An aneurysm is a saclike protrusion of an artery caused by a weakened area within the vessel wall. If a cerebral aneurysm ruptures, the escaping blood within the brain may cause severe neurological complications and/

or death. A person with a ruptured cerebral aneurysm may complain of the sudden onset of the worst headache of his or her life, may complain of a popping sensation in the head, a stiff neck, loss of vision, or nausea. The individual may begin vomiting and have a seizure. This injured athlete needs to be transported to the nearest trauma center immediately.

Diagnosis for this condition is confirmed with a CT of the brain, a lumbar puncture to test for CSF in blood, and angiogram, or an MRI of the brain. Treatment options include surgery or coiling to stop bleeding, placement of a ventricular catheter in the ventricles of the brain to drain fluid and relieve the cranial pressure.(Mayfield) Vasospasm and hypertension also needs to be closely monitored and controlled.

SECOND IMPACT SYNDROME

In 1973, neurosurgeon R. C. Schneider and his colleagues presented a clinical case of an athlete who died from a second blow to the head before recovering fully from the initial concussion. This condition has been termed second-impact syndrome (qtd. in Cantu).

Second-impact syndrome is a condition that occurs when an athlete who has sustained a head injury—usually a concussion or cerebral contusion—sustains a second head injury before symptoms associated with the first injury have cleared. This condition creates accumulative neurologic and cognitive deficits, such as in the cases of many boxers and football players. If the recurrent trauma occurs within a short period of time (hours, days, weeks) and there is repeated head trauma with probable concussions that may be considered mild, accumulative injuries can be fatal. There needs to be more research to prove clearly these catastrophic injuries were solely due to repetitive head trauma.

Bleeding or swelling in the brain can cause pressure that forces the brain downward in the skull, which causes a herniation. The most common type of herniation is a transtentorial herniation, where the temporal lobe is forced through the tentorial notch (Maiese). The pupil of the eye dilates and may not constrict in response to light. A transtentorial herniation can cause paralysis, stupor, coma, abnormal heart rhythms, disturbance or cessation of breathing, cardiac arrest, and death.

As the injured brain bleeds or swells, this increases the pressure on the brain, because there is nowhere for it to go within the confines of the skull. As the pressure increases, the athlete's symptoms increase. The athlete will complain of sensitivity to light, increased headache, confusion, nausea, and vomiting; he or she may lose consciousness. The herniation can cause a coma or death, as the vital portion of the brain stem—which controls heart rate and breathing—is compromised.

When an athlete has sustained a traumatic brain injury, the brain may be injured in a specific location, or the injury may be diffused to many parts of the brain. It is important to understand that the brain coordinates its different parts to function as a whole.

The portion of the brain injured can reveal particular deficits or abnormalities. The cerebral cortex is located in the frontal lobe, under the forehead. The cerebral cortex is responsible for our awareness of our surroundings and controls emotional responses, our expressive language, and memory for habits and motor activities. Injury to the cerebral cortex could cause paralysis, inability to multitask, inability to focus, persistence of a single thought, mood changes, personality changes, inability to express language, and difficulty with problem solving.

The parietal lobe, located near the back of the brain and on top of the head, assists us with visual attention, touch perception, and integrating thought processes for understanding a single concept. An injury to the parietal lobe would make it difficult to attend to more than one task at a time, name an object, locate words for writing, read, and draw. It also makes it difficult to distinguish the left side from the right side. It shows deficits in eye-hand coordination, lack of awareness of certain body parts, and an inability to focus visual attention.

The occipital lobe is at the back of the head and is primarily responsible for vision. An injury to the occipital lobe would lead to difficulty locating objects in the environment, difficulty identifying colors, possible hallucinations, an inability to recognize movement of an object, and difficulty reading and writing.

The temporal lobes are located on the sides of the head, just above the ears. They are responsible for hearing, memory, visual perception, and categorization of objects. An injury to a temporal lobe could result in difficulties in recognizing faces, understanding spoken words, and identifying objects, as well as short-term memory loss, long-term memory loss, inability to categorize objects, and an increase in aggressive behavior. Damage to the right lobe can cause persistent talking.

The brain stem is located deep in the brain, and it controls breathing, heart rate, swallowing, visual and auditory components sweating, blood pressure, and temperature regulation, and it affects the level of alertness, the ability to sleep, and the sense of balance. A brain stem injury can cause dizziness, breathing problems, speech problems, difficulty swallowing, balance problems, and insomnia.

The cerebellum is located at the base of the skull and is responsible for equilibrium. An injury to the cerebellum can cause an inability to coordinate fine movements, make rapid movements, walk, and reach out and grab objects. An injury may also cause tremors and slurred speech.

Location of the swelling and/or pressure on the brain explains the huge difference in how an athlete responds following a traumatic brain injury (concussion). I have seen some athletes become extremely emotional and cry. Others become angry, shove you away, and have personality changes. Some react by laughing constantly; they think every question you ask is hysterically funny. I was working a football game several years ago, and the referee brought a kid off of the field and said, "This kid's in trouble." The ref said he blew his whistle to start the play, and this athlete walked up to him and asked, "Lunchtime; did you bring your lunch?" When I evaluated this kid, he sang the answer to every question, and he laughed at everything.

Recent research reveals a correlation with genetic factors and the significance of apolipoprotein (Apo) Ey (APO E). APO E promotes gene, tau polymerase, and other genetic markers that may be possible reasons for increased effects of a head trauma. Evidence from human and animal studies of more severe traumatic brain injury shows induction of a variety of genetic and cytokine factors, such as insulin-like growth factor-1 (IGF-1), IGF binding protein-2, fibroblast growth factor, Cu-Zn superoxide dismutase, superoxide dismutase-1(SOD-1), and nerve growth factor glial fibrillary acidic proteins (GFAP and S100)(Peng et al.). More research on this correlation needs to be performed

CHAPTER 2

ASSESSMENT OF HEAD INJURY: SIGNS/SYMPTOMS, SIDELINE EVALUATION VS. CLINICAL EVALUATION

Proper documentation and initial assessment of head and/or neck trauma are essential to the subsequent management of the injury. There are more than twenty-five recognized guidelines for the assessment and management of concussion. I have included several of these assessment tools for your review. I have also included one of the assessment tools I utilize in my own sports injury practice as an additional tool.

Sports medicine professionals are continuously searching for standardized methods to obtain a more objective evaluation of head trauma. These methods assist the athletic trainer/physician to quantify the severity of injury and measure the athlete's progress as he or she recovers. Data from objective measures of cognitive function, postural stability, and post-concussion signs and symptoms are most helpful in making a determination about severity of injury and post injury recovery. An emerging model of sport concussion assessment involves the use of brief screening tools to evaluate post-concussion signs and symptoms, cognitive function, and postural stability on the sideline immediately after an injury in conjunction with physical exam of the athlete.

The assessment of a head/neck injury begins with a thorough history. The following questions are important to ask: Have you ever had any previous trauma to your head/neck? If so, when? Was there loss of consciousness? If yes, for how long? How many head-/neck-related traumas have you had?

What treatment was rendered? Did you have a CT scan/MRI? What were the results of the CT, MRI, or other imaging studies? How long did you sit out of sports participation post-concussion? Did you have any related problems after returning to sports participation? How long did it take for your signs/symptoms to resolve completely? Have you had any fractures or surgery on your face, head, or neck? Do you have any known congenital conditions of your head, neck, or brain?

You need to take a specific history for each episode of head/neck trauma. These questions should also be included on the preseason sports participation physical form, and any history should be placed on the athlete's emergency medical card, along with allergies, past illnesses, known conditions, meds, emergency contact information, and so on. This information can be very useful to the sports medicine professional.

When an injury occurs during an athletic event, the athlete is typically dazed and unable to recall this information. The sports medicine professional can pull out the emergency medical card from the training kit and obtain any history the athlete is unable to recall as a result of confusion or amnesia caused by the injury.

Some of you probably remember playing and getting hit in the head and the coach simply asked you to say how many fingers he or she was holding up. If you answered correctly, you were returned to play. We now know this is not an adequate assessment technique for sports concussion. There is no such thing as a simple "ding" to the head.

The initial sideline evaluation should include determination that a head or neck injury has occurred and whether the athlete needs to be transported immediately for further evaluation. The athlete should be evaluated for level of consciousness, steadiness of gait, orientation, and posttraumatic amnesia. The sports medicine staff should have an emergency medical plan in place and should have practiced it prior to the beginning of the season.

The initial assessment of a traumatic injury to the head or neck includes the following:

- assessing ABCs (airway, breathing, circulation) to determine whether to call 911
- questioning athlete to determine mental status
- motor and sensory testing and balance evaluation

A set of orientation questions that aids in determining whether an athlete has sustained a concussion are known as "Maddocks Questions."

Dr. D. L. Maddocks and colleagues developed this qualitative measurement of screenings for mental abnormalities, and they are useful for determining the presence of a concussion and need for further assessment.

Maddocks Questions include the following:
Which field are we at?
Which team are we playing today?
Who is your opponent?
Which quarter/period is it in the game?
Which team scored the last point/touchdown/goal in the game?
What team did you play last week?
Who won the game last week?

Other assessment tools include the SAC, which was designed in response to and in accordance with the American Academy of Neurology's Practice Parameter for Concussion (1997), an enhanced version of the 1991 Colorado guidelines for the management of concussion in sports. Dr. Michael McCrea and colleagues introduced the SAC in 1998. The SAC(Standardized Assessment of Concussion) includes a standard, brief measure of orientation, concentration, delayed recall, and neurological screening. It assesses strength, coordination, sensation, and the presence of amnesia. Functional maneuvers (including sit-ups and knee bends) are also included. This test is given preseason to obtain a baseline score and then performed at the time of injury, and the two scores are compared.

The University of Pittsburgh Medical Center's Sports Concussion Program has developed a brief mental status exam called Impact and has published a "concussion card" for sideline use by sports medicine professionals.

Another recent sideline assessment tools is the Sports Concussion Assessment Tool (SCAT). The SCAT is a compilation of a condensed form of existing evaluations that are completed by the sports medicine professional and the athlete. It includes a symptom checklist, concentration tests, mental status tasks, and neurological screening. SCAT has been enhanced by SCAT 2.

Concussion Sentinel is a computer test that compares a baseline test to post injury results. Concussion Sentinel provides the two key components of preseason preparation:

1. A concussion history taken while the athlete is healthy provides important baseline information in the event of a concussion. When an athlete has a history of previous concussions, physicians/providers should proceed with extra caution when making return-to-play decisions.

2. Concussion causes subtle changes in the speed and accuracy of cognition (thinking ability). These changes are usually the last symptoms to go away after a concussion. They can be very slight, making it more difficult to detect without a computer test that compares an individual to their before-trauma status. This means testing before the injury occurs is helpful

What I have discovered from my experience as a sports medicine professional is that most high schools barely have the financial availability to provide an athletic trainer for the school and certainly do not have the finances to purchase computer testing for their athletes. For that reason, I designed a written cognitive test and had athletes participating in contact sports take this test prior to the season, post injury, and one to two weeks post concussion. This has served as a helpful tool and is not time consuming or expensive.

Some of the other assessment tools appear to be comprehensive and helpful but are not practical for clinical use. For example, what team physician or certified athletic trainer is going to take the time to have the injured athlete fill out a questionnaire or take a computer test on the sideline when this athlete may have just taken a hit, lost consciousness, or is confused and complaining of a severe headache and nausea? Our main concern at that point is to make sure this athlete gets prompt medical attention, especially when the game has continued and there are another three or four athletes coming to us with injuries that need evaluated. High schools and small colleges, which are where the majority of catastrophic injuries occur, have limited staff to assist with sports medicine coverage.

Another problem is that at the state and world-class events I cover as a team physician, there is no opportunity to do a baseline, pre-injury test, and we most often do not know anything about these athletes and their medical histories. I recently attended a pep rally before a postseason college Football bowl game. A band member was struck with one of the flagpoles during this event, and her wrist swelled twice its size instantly. There was no trainer with the more than three hundred-member band, nor did they have a medical kit or bag with them. They did not have a medical card on this young girl, whose parents were fourteen hours away. I asked the local policeman at the event to call for a squad, and we obtained ice at a local restaurant. I applied pressure to the area and splinted it until medical help arrived, which took over twenty minutes. I thought, *I am certainly glad this was not a serious concussion or life-threatening injury.*

I believe all teams, bands, cheerleading squads, and so on should have to follow a standard of care. We require our coaches to attend certification classes, yet there is no requirement to keep a medical card on athletes or to have a medical kit at practices, games, and events. This is why I have reviewed all of the available assessment tools and tried to design a better standardization of care for athletes with concussions or other head injuries. Getting prompt care immediately to an athlete who has sustained a serious head trauma could be a matter of life and death. A prime example is the development of the AED (Automated External Defibrillator) for acute heart conditions. This machine evaluates the hearts status, gives instant feedback on what is going on, and provides step-by-step instructions about what needs to be done for the person in distress. This is what needs to be designed to evaluate the seriousness of concussion and head trauma. There needs to be a standard evaluation that all providers—sports injury physicians, athletic trainers, pediatricians, family practitioners, neurologists, and so on—use in making return-to-play decisions.

As a team physician, I use a variety of assessment tools. If I am working with one of my teams for which I have preseason testing information, I use my own cognitive test, which is similar to the SCAT 2 test. But if I am covering a national event, where I do not know the athletes, I may utilize Maddocks. And if I am covering a college event, where they may have impact testing and preseason baseline test results on that athlete, I obtain the information from the certified athletic trainer at that particular university and ask for a post injury test to be performed.

The National Athletic Trainers Association (NATA) position statement on sports-related concussion (Guskiewicz et al.) strongly recommends the use of balance testing as part of the baseline and postconcussion assessment. Other assessment tools include testing the cranial nerves; performing the Romberg test or Bess test, which is a quantitative version of a modified Romberg test for balance; grip strength; and neurological testing, including sensory and motor function.

Once the athlete has been properly evaluated, the sports medicine professional must decide on the best course of management for the athlete, which is clearly not easy. This decision must not rely solely on the physical exam. As we discussed earlier, signs/symptoms do not always show up immediately. This decision should be based on history of head or neck trauma and the potential for further injury, along with exam findings.

AN ATHLETE WHO HAS THE FOLLOWING SHOULD BE TRANSPORTED TO THE HOSPITAL FOR FURTHER NEUROLOGIC TESTING AND/OR IMAGING

(Situations in italics require the athlete be transported to the nearest ER department *immediately*.)

*loss of consciousness on the field/court

*amnesia lasting longer than fifteen minutes

deterioration of neurologic function

decreasing level of consciousness

decrease or irregularity in respirations

decrease or irregularity in pulse

unequal, dilated, or unreactive pupils

any signs or symptoms of associated injuries, spine or skull fracture, or bleeding

changes in mental status: lethargy, difficulty maintaining arousal, confusion, or unusual agitation

seizure activity

*vomiting

*increase in blood pressure

*motor deficits subsequent to initial on field assessment

*cranial nerve deficits

*sensory deficits subsequent to initial on field assessment

*balance deficits subsequent to initial on field assessment

*cranial nerve deficits subsequent to initial on field assessment

*post concussion symptoms that worsen

*additional post concussion symptoms as compared with those on the field

*symptoms still present at end of game (especially at high school level)

DELAYED REFERRAL (after the day of injury)

*any of the findings in the day of injury referral category

*post concussion symptoms that worsen or do not improve over time

*increase in the number of post concussion symptoms reported

*post concussion symptoms that begin to interfere with the athlete's daily activities (sleep or cognitive disturbances)

("Physician")

If there is ever a question about transporting an athlete with a head trauma, you should transport! Send a copy of the athlete's emergency medical card along with your on field evaluation form (a sample of this form appears at the end of this chapter) with the paramedic or parent to give to ER physician Also give the parent a head injury sheet, which lists signs/symptoms and instructions about how to care for the athlete post trauma, instructing them to observe the athlete carefully for the next twenty-four to forty-eight hours.

Below is the Roush Sport On-field Assessment Test, which I designed.

As stated previously, it evaluates both the head and neck simultaneously and includes return-to-play guidelines based on a comprehensive review of the athlete's history, physical exam findings, balance testing, cognitive testing, and physical activity testing. It can be administered on the sideline with ease and in a timely manner. This assessment test gives precise instructions about when you should make a referral and when you can move on to the next portion of the exam. It is as simple as marking a plus or minus to determine function.

ROUSH

Sports Concussion Practitioner On-Field Evaluation and Return-to-Play Test

Designed by Dr. Kelly J. Roush, CCSP, ATC

*This evaluation process shall serve as a guideline for making return-to-play decisions, but a final decision to return to play must be determined by using all tools of assessment combined with the physical exam.

Scoring of this test is determined by the following:
Please mark a plus sign (+) by any section of the test where listed signs/symptoms are present or an abnormal finding is determined.

Please mark a minus sign (–) sign by any section of the test where signs/symptoms are *not* present or all findings are normal.

*All testing (#1–#13) should be performed with cervical spine immobilized.

1. *Signs/Symptoms:* please circle all s/s the athlete has at time of examination.

   _____ Headache/dizziness/nausea/vomiting/blurred vision/ ringing in ears/numbness or weakness of any body part/ radiating pain to arms or legs/spinal pain/confusion/clear fluid oozing form the nose or ears/memory loss/ erotic behavior

   _____ Mechanism of Injury: What happened? Did you take a blow to the head and/or neck

Where is your pain? headache only or head and neck pain? How would you describe your pain? Sharp, tingling, throbbing, burning, etc.

2. *Airway, Breathing, Circulation:*

   _____ Is normal and remains normal throughout the entire exam process

   If compromised, *no return to play!* Call EMS and provide emergency procedures.

3. *Testing of Pupils:* pupils are equal and reactive to light.

   _____ Direct: (constricted/dilated/unreactive)

   _____Consensual Response: (constricted/dilated/unreactive)

4. *Cardinal Fields of Vision:*

   _____ Normal in all fields. List which fields are abnormal _____Nystagmus? Yes/No

5. *State of Alertness:*

   _____Athlete has no amnesia and is aware of person, place, and time

   Ask the athlete his or her name, his or her location, who the opponent is, the day of the week, who they played last week, who won the game last week, what his or her jersey number is, the name of the coach, if he or she knows who you are, to recite the days of the week backward, and to remember a number/color sequence. Have the athlete memorize this sequence (7-orange-23-apple in order) and repeat back to you throughout the evaluation process.

6. *History of Concussion* (found on emergency medical card):

   _____ Athlete has no previously diagnosed concussion or signs/symptoms of a concussion in the past year and has never lost consciousness. If there is a prior injury, list date, and if there was a loss of consciousness (LOC), indicate how long it took to be cleared. Were they evaluated by a physician? Was any special testing performed (CT/MRI)?

7. *History of Skull/Spinal Conditions* (found on emergency medical card):

_____ Athlete has no predisposing skull and/or spinal malformations/conditions, such as spinal stenosis, cervical disk herniation, past fractures, Klippel-Feil Syndrome, and Arnold-Chiari malformation.

8. *Palpation:*

_____ No palpable abnormality/no pain over spine.

If abnormality detected, list location _____.

9. *Radicular Pain:*

_____ Does athlete have any radicular pain to upper or lower extremity, face, jaw, and so on?

If so, to where does the pain radiate?

10. *Sensory Testing:*

_____ Sensory testing is normal in all four quadrants.

If abnormal, what dermatome is abnormal?

11. *Motor Testing:*

_____ Athlete has full motor testing in all 4 quadrants

If abnormal, at what level?_____

12. *Strength Testing:*

_____ Athlete has full grip strength in both hands.

_____ Athlete can independently move his or her hands and feet (keep cervical spine immobilized).

_____ Athlete has full strength in plantar flexion and dorsiflexion of the ankle.

If all tests, 1–12, are normal, keep cervical spine immobilized and bring athlete to a seated position. If no new signs/symptoms arise, continue with exam.

13. *Testing of Cranial Nerves:*

    _____ Cranial nerves are intact. If abnormality is detected, list which tests are abnormal_____.

14. *Reflexes:*

    ____plantar   ____patella   ___achilles

    ____biceps   ____triceps

    ____brachioradialis

15. *Active Cervical Range of Motion:*

    _____ Athlete has full range of motion (ROM) in flexion/extension/lateral flexion/rotation of the cervical spine with no spinal pain. Evaluate for cervical muscle strain vs. spinal condition.

    If no pain with active ROM, remove the athlete from the field and complete evaluation.

16. *Cervical Tests:*

    _____Resistive ROM testing in cervical flexion, extension, right and left lateral flexion and right and left rotation, Spurling's Test,

17. *Coordination:*

    _____ *Romberg's Test:* If the athlete has negative Romberg's test at rest with verbal commands, ask athlete to keep eyes closed and raise right arm above head, left arm out to the side. Then ask the athlete to switch positions. Give four to five series of verbal commands to move the arms while standing with heels together and eyes closed. If the athlete sways or if the arms have trouble finding neutral position, the test is positive. Also, evaluate if the athlete is having difficulty following commands.

_____ Finger to nose test

18. *Tandem Walk:*

_____ Athlete can do tandem walk with no balance problems and/or dizziness.

19. *Visual Ability and Sensitivity to Light*:

_____ Athlete can look at scoreboard and tell you what the score is without squinting. If the athlete cannot focus or the lights bother his or her eyes, the test is positive.

20. *Vitals:*

_____ Blood pressure and pulse are normal for patient (compare recording of vitals from sports physical on emergency medical card). If no emergency medical card, blood pressure must be under 140/90. BP_____
Pulse_____   Respirations_____

*A high pulse pressure (systolic minus diastolic > 60 mmHg) immediately following exercise should restore itself within ten minutes post-exercise. If the pulse pressure remains high and the pulse rate is tremendously lower than that expected following exercise, the athlete may have increased intracranial pressure, possibly from a brain hemorrhage.

*If there are any plus (+) marks on the evaluation process #1 through #20, the athlete is *not* returned to play and is to be reevaluated (except for history portion, #6 and 7, of the process) every five minutes and monitored closely; the athlete is *never to be left alone.*

*If there are all minus signs (–) on the evaluation process #1 through #20, you may proceed to the functional exam.

FUNCTIONAL EXAM

_____ Athlete can jog forward twenty feet with no signs/symptoms of concussion.

_____ Athlete can jog backward twenty feet with no signs/symptoms of concussion.

_____ Athlete can squat five times with hands above head with no signs/symptoms of concussion.

_____Athlete can do side shuffles (three time to each side for approximately ten feet) with no signs/symptoms of concussion.

_____Athlete can do ten push-ups with no signs/symptoms of concussion.

_____ Athlete can do ten jumping jacks with no signs/symptoms of concussion.

List any signs/symptoms of concussion and/or neck injury (headache, dizziness, and so on):

Observe airway, breathing, and circulation, and repeat testing of pupil reactiveness, cardinal fields of vision, Romberg's test, and cognitive awareness questions (person, place, time). Ask the athlete to recite the memorization sequence you gave him or her earlier, repeat sensory and motor testing, grip strength testing, tandem walk, and any positive finding from prior exam.

*If the athlete's post exercise test is normal, the first portion of the evaluation process and it has been determined that there is no probable concussion, the athlete may return to play but must be observed closely and reevaluated throughout the contest and after the game. Parents must be made aware of possible concussion and given a head injury sheet.

*If the athlete develops symptomatology or starts showing signs of concussion, take him or her *out* of the athletic participation and do not allow him or her to return the same day. Consider ER referral.

*If the athlete has abnormality on functional exam but condition is stable, reevaluate every five minutes.

*Have the athlete perform a cognitive/neuropsychological test immediately after the competition/game.

*The athlete should be evaluated by a physician within twenty-four to forty-eight hours post injury and should *not* participate in any physical activity until evaluated by a sports specialty physician and/or neurologist if a concussion is diagnosed.

Description of Testing for Each Component of the ROUSH Sport Practitioner On-Field and Return-to-Play and Evaluation Test

1. *Signs/Symptoms*

   Ask what the athlete is feeling while observing mood and alertness.

2. *Airway, Breathing, Circulation*

   Palpate pulse while observing chest rises. If the athlete is wearing a helmet, keep it on, cut the face mask, and flip up without moving the head and/or neck. Only remove the helmet if the face mask cannot be removed and breathing is compromised.

3. *Testing of Pupils*

   Direct: Carefully note each pupil's size. Check the athlete's eyes with a penlight. Shine the light directly into one pupil as the athlete keeps the other eye closed. Note the reaction of the pupil. Then check the other eye.

   Normal: Pupils constrict and remain constricted with light; pupils dilate when light is removed.

   Consensual Response: The athlete keeps both eyes open. Position the penlight directly in front of the athlete's right eye. Turn on the penlight, and observe the reaction of the left pupil. Then check the other eye.

   Normal: Pupils constrict bilaterally and remain constricted with light.

4. *Cardinal Fields of Vision* (Extraocular Eye Movement):

   Ask the athlete to follow your finger's movement in an "H" pattern with his or her eyes without moving the head. Then slowly move your finger to your right and then to your left. When your finger is approximately twenty-four inches (60 cm) from your starting point, or the athlete's eye movement stops (in either or both eyes), hold it still. Note the position of the iris in relation to each eye's midline. Repeat this procedure, checking each vision field separately.

Normal: Eyes move smoothly and bilaterally in six cardinal fields of gaze.

Abnormal finding in oculomotor (III) nerve damage: lid ptosis, with inability to open the eye completely, eyeball deviated outward and slightly downward, pupil dilated and unreactive to light, nystagmus, and accommodation power lost

Abnormal findings in trochlear IV nerve damage: inability to turn eye downward or outward

Abnormal findings in abducen VI nerve damage: eyeball deviated inward, diplopia, paralysis of lateral gaze

Possible Causes of Abnormalities

Trauma, aneurysm at base of skull, increased intracranial pressure, multiple sclerosis, tumor, botulism, or lead poisoning

5. *State of Alertness*

   This evaluation component consists of a series of questions and tasks, such as recalling events, making sure the athlete is aware of who he or she is, where the athlete is, and what time frame it is (day of week, month of the year, quarter of the ball game). Ask the athlete to complete a line of a common nursery rhyme, such as, "Jack and Jill went up the hill to fetch a pail of _____."

6. *History of Concussion/Skull/Spinal Condition*

   Ask the athlete about any previous concussion and loss of consciousness. When was the last concussion? Have someone get the athlete's emergency medical card from the training kit and tell you what it says under past concussion/spinal history.

*If the athlete has had a concussion in the past month with or without loss of consciousness, and/or has spinal pain or any radicular pain or any sensory or motor deficits, he or she *cannot* be cleared to return to play.

*If the athlete has had a concussion in the past six months with loss of consciousness, or took longer than one week to recover fully, or has spinal pain with or without radicular complaint, he or she *cannot* be cleared to return to play.

*If the athlete has had a concussion in the past six months and there was no loss of consciousness and the athlete fully recovered within one week, has no spinal pain, has no radiculopathy, has no sensory or motor deficits, has full cervical ROM, has no memory loss, has normal balance, and has no increase in symptomology post exertion test, the athlete may consider returning to play.

7. *Palpation*

If the athlete is wearing a helmet, keep it on and palpate the area of complaint, starting away from the point of pain. For example, if the athlete says, "My upper neck hurts," start palpation at the upper thoracic spine and move toward the upper neck. Feel for any deformity, spasm, or warmth. Palpation should be performed while the head is immobilized, and neck motion should be minimized.

8. *Radicular Pain*

Ask the athlete if there is any pain radiating to the arms or legs or into the face or head.

9. *Sensory Testing*

Sensory nerves carry information about sensations such as touch, pain, heat, cold, vibration, position, and shape from the body to the brain. Abnormal sensations or decreased perception of sensations may indicate damage to a sensory nerve, the spinal cord, or certain parts of the brain.

Test the athlete in all dermatomes bilaterally, asking the athlete to tell you where he or she feels your touch, while the athlete keeps his or her head still. The area of decreased sensation can give you an idea of what level of the spine might be injured:

Shoulder: C6

Inner and outer forearm: C6, T1

Thumb and little finger: C6, C8

Front of both thighs: L2

Medial, lateral calves: L4, L5

Little toes: S1

10. *Motor Testing*

Motor nerves carry impulses from the brain and spinal cord to voluntary muscles. Weakness or paralysis of a muscle may indicate damage to the muscle, brain, or spinal cord. Observe the athlete for muscle twitching, tremor, pattern of weakness, and muscle tone. If the muscle is flaccid immediately post trauma, it could indicate spinal cord injury. An injury to the thoracic spine could cause the legs, but not the arms, to be paralyzed. An injury in or above the neck can cause paralysis of all four limbs. Motor testing should be performed with as little movement of the spine as possible.

Grading System

0/5: no muscle movement

1/5: visible muscle movement, but no movement at the joint

2/5: movement at a joint but not against gravity

3/5: movement at a joint but not with added resistance

4/5: movement against resistance but less than normal

5/5: normal

Motor Testing Levels

Flexion at elbow: C5, C6 (biceps)

Extension at elbow: C6, C7, C8 (triceps)

Wrist extension: C6, C7, C 8 (radial)

Finger abduction: C8, T1 (ulnar)

Opposition of thumb: C8, T1 (median)

Hip flexion: L2, L3, L4 (iliopsoas)

Knee extension: L2, L3, L4 (quads)

Knee flexion: L4, S1, S2 (hamstrings)

Ankle dorsiflexion: L4, L5

Ankle plantar flexion: S1

11. *Strength Training*

    Test the athlete's grip strength bilaterally and then ask him or her to push the toes against your hand (plantar flexion) and up toward the body (ankle dorsiflexion) against the resistance of your hand, with no movement of the neck or spine.

*If spinal injury is not suspected, the athlete may be taken to sideline for further testing.

12. *Testing of Cranial Nerves*

    You tested cranial nerves III, IV, and VI when you tested cardinal fields of vision.

    Cranial nerve I olfactory (sense of smell) and II (optic) may be difficult to test on the sideline.

    Cranial nerve V can be tested by evaluating sensations in the face and scalp. Have the athlete clench his or her teeth while you palpate the masseter muscles bilaterally, feeling for bulging of the muscles as the teeth are clenched. Jaw reflex is a good indicator of increased tone. Central nervous system (CNS) lesions will likely involve all three divisions of CN V. Peripheral nervous system (PNS) lesions can involve one or more of the branches. An upper motor neuron lesion (UMNL) will produce little dysfunction due to bilateral innervation to the muscles of mastication. A lower motor neuron lesion (LMNL) will result in paralysis and atrophy of mastication muscles.

27

Cranial nerve VII can be tested through taste and facial expressions.

Cranial nerve IX is tested using the posterior portion of the tongue.

Cranial nerve VII requires testing of the anterior portion of the tongue.

1. Instruct the patient to identify familiar liquids (sugar water, salt water, lemon juice) placed on tongue with a sterile cotton swab or sterile medicine dropper. Test anterior two-thirds by placing two to three drops of liquid on each side of the anterior portion of the tongue and then on the posterior portion of the tongue.

*Make sure you do not use any material to which the athlete may be allergic (peanut butter, for example).

2. Instruct the athlete to smile and frown. Observe for asymmetry of muscle tone of the face.

*Abnormality could indicate a PNS lesion, resulting in weakness in ipsilateral facial muscles and loss of taste from ipsilateral anterior two-thirds of the tongue.

*A PNS lesion is different than a CNS dysfunction. An athlete with a CNS lesion will retain the ability to wrinkle the forehead or raise the eyebrows.

*Cortical lesions are contralateral.

*Brain stem lesions are ipsilateral.

Cranial nerve VIII involves the vestibulocochlear nerve.

Testing of this cranial nerve includes: Hearing/lateralization/air and bone conduction/vestibular

Cranial Nerves IX and X (glossopharyngeal and vagus nerves) control palatal reflex, gag reflex, hoarseness of voice, and motor function. The athlete may complain of difficulty swallowing.

*Observe for intact gag reflex, symmetrical palatal reflex, and normal clarity of speech with normal motor function.

Equipment: tongue depressor

Cranial nerve XI is an accessory nerve. It is evaluated by manual muscle testing of trapezius and sternocleidomastoid muscles.

Cranial Nerve XII is the hypoglossal nerve.

Evaluate tongue movements and tongue strength.

*Damage to an upper motor neuron will result in tongue deviation to the same side as the lesion.

*Dysfunction causing tongue weakness can occur from cerebral infarction or metastatic tumor(Pociask

*Observe for tongue symmetry without atrophy or tremor.

13. Reflexes

A reflex is an automatic response to a stimulus. The pathway consists of the sensory nerve to the spinal cord, the nerve connections in the spinal cord, and the motor nerves back to the muscle.

Plantar Reflex

Firmly stroke the outer border of the sole of the foot with a blunt object. The toes should curl downward (except in infants). The test is abnormal if the toe goes up and the other toes spread. It may indicate an abnormality in the brain or spinal cord.

Biceps: C5, C6

Triceps: C6, C7

Brachioradialis: C5, C6

Abdominal: T8–T12

Knee: L2–L4

Achilles: S1, S2

Tendon Reflex Grading System

0: Absent

1+: Hypoactive

2+: Normal

3+: Hyperactive without clonus

4+: Hyperactive with clonus

14. Active Cervical Range of Motion

Ask the athlete to move the neck *slowly* into flexion, extension, lateral flexion, and rotation. Movement should be stopped if there is any pain. Compare the amount of lateral flexion and rotation side to side. Then you may test passive range of motion. *Always test active ROM first!*

15. Cervical Tests (test in a seated position):

Resistive ROM: If active ROM was pain free, ask the athlete to perform all ROM of the cervical spine. Add slight resistance to each motion, asking the athlete to tell you if he or she has any pain. Pain on the opposite side of rotation could indicate cervical strain, and pain on the same side of rotation could indicate an impingement or spinal condition.

Valsalva: Ask the athlete to cough, sneeze, or bear down like he or she is having a bowel movement. Where does the athlete have pain?

Spurling's Test: The result is positive if there is pain with maneuver.

16. Coordination

Romberg's Test: This test evaluates proprioception and pathway function. It is used to investigate the cause of motor coordination loss (ataxia). A positive Romberg's test suggests the ataxia is sensory in nature, depending on the loss of proprioception. If a patient is ataxic and Romberg's test is not positive, it suggests the ataxia is cerebellar in nature, depending on localized cerebellar dysfunction. Look for swaying. You must stay close to the athlete to steady him or her in case of loss of balance.

Finger to Nose Test: Ask the athlete to touch your hand and then his or her nose alternately several times. Move your hand about as the athlete performs this task.

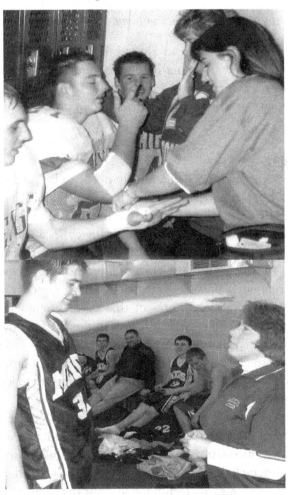

17. Tandem Stance

Have the athlete stand heel to toe with non dominant foot in back. Weight should be evenly distributed across both feet. The athlete should try to maintain this stance for twenty seconds, with hands on hips and eyes closed. If the athlete stumbles out of position, the test is positive.

18. Tandem Walk

Ask the athlete to walk heel to toe for about ten feet. Observe any unsteadiness, which indicates possible ataxia.

19. Visual Ability and Sensitivity to Light

Ask the athlete to read the score on the scoreboard or something like a banner he or she should be able to focus on with ease. Observe if the athlete squints due to light sensitivity or complains of blurred vision or flashes of light.

Special Imaging

If it has been determined the athlete needs to be further evaluated, he or she will be transported to the ER by squad. The ER physician will most likely order a special study to determine the seriousness of the head injury. The special imaging ordered is typically either a CT scan or MRI of the brain. These methods of neuroimaging evaluate structural damage and are used to rule out the presence of a brain bleed. These structural tests do *not* rule out a possible concussion. They only help determine if a life-threatening condition is present that needs prompt neurosurgical attention. An athlete will typically be seen in the ER after the head/neck trauma has occurred, have a CT or MRI of the brain—which is most often read as normal—and the athlete returns home that same day. Open MRIs should not be used, as the resolution is insufficient to identify brain injury ("Traumatic").

Other types of neuroimaging include functional MRI, which indirectly measures oxygen utilization; PET scan (positron emission tomography), which measures glucose utilization; and SPECT (single photon emission computed tomography), which measures blood flow in the brain. PET scanning is the best imaging technique to assist in the diagnosis of subtle brain injury, because it is a functional imaging test and very sensitive to the diffuse changes seen after concussion ("Traumatic").

Again I stress that a normal CT scan or normal MRI does *not* mean the athlete does not have a concussion. It means there was no acute structural problem or bleed found on that particular film. If the athlete's condition deteriorates or post concussion symptoms begin to interfere with daily activities, take the athlete back to the ER for further evaluation.

CT scan is the best choice of imaging for an acute (recent head trauma) of the head and face, bleeding in the brain (within the first 24 to 48 hours), skull bone disorders or early symptoms of stroke. CT is typically performed if there is loss of consciousness longer than 5 seconds, concern that a skull fracture may be present or any evidence of a focal neurologic deficit. ("Concussions")

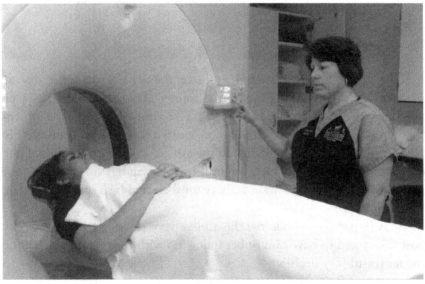

In one study, 209 of 1,538 patients with normal neurological exams were found to have abnormalities on CT, with 58 requiring neurosurgery (Stein and Ross).

If there is a positive finding on the athlete's CT scan of the brain and/ or if the athlete's condition worsens, the ER may send the athlete to a trauma center for further evaluation, or the ER physician may decide to keep the athlete in the hospital for observation. Most athletes have normal CT scans and are sent home with a head injury sheet and instructions to the parent to watch him or her closely for the next twenty-four to seventy-two hours.

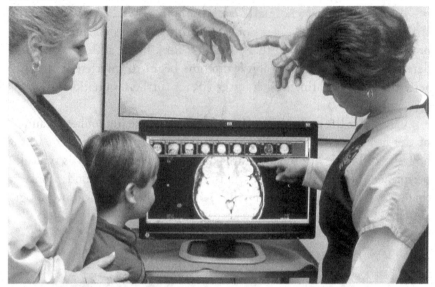

The athletic trainer should evaluate the athlete the next day at practice or in the training room. The trainer may perform cognitive or neuropsychological testing, such as SCAT2 or impact testing. The athlete should be monitored closely and follow written instructions from the ER physician. You should emphasize to the athlete that he or she should not only avoid sports activity but also limit text messaging, video games, and any activity that stresses brain activity until cleared by a sports physician to return to play.

It is imperative to observe the athlete very closely for several weeks post injury and to have him or her follow up with the team physician for the return-to-play decision.

CHAPTER 3

GRADES OF CONCUSSION/RETURN-TO-PLAY DECISIONS/TREATMENT OPTIONS FOR BRAIN BLEEDS

Over the past twenty years, there have been multiple classifications for management of sports-related concussion. In recent years, the three concussion classifications systems most widely used are the Cantu Grading System, which emphasizes memory disturbance or amnesia; the Colorado Guidelines; and the the system devised by the American Academy of Neurology, which emphasizes loss of consciousness.

Cantu Grading System

Grade Signs/Symptoms

1 Mild   no loss of consciousness
                  posttraumatic amnesia < 30 min

2 Moderate   loss of consciousness <5 min
                  posttraumatic amnesia >30 min but <24 hours in
duration

3 Severe   loss of consciousness >5 min
                  posttraumatic amnesia >24 hours

Colorado Medical Society Guidelines

Grade Signs/Symptoms
1 Mild confusion without amnesia
no loss of consciousness

2 Moderate confusion with amnesia
no loss of consciousness

3 Severe loss of consciousness

American Academy of Neurology Guidelines

1 Mild transient confusion
no loss of consciousness
symptoms/abnormalities resolve <15 min

2 Moderate transient confusion
no loss of consciousness
symptoms/abnormalities resolve >15 min

3 Severe any loss of consciousness, either brief (seconds) or prolonged (minutes)

These grading systems are helpful but not conclusive. When determining the seriousness of a concussion and making return-to-play decisions, a physician must use these guidelines in conjunction with the physical exam, history, and other assessment tools.

Treatment

Treatment is determined by the type of head/neck injury. Until a neck injury is ruled out, any athlete suspected of a head injury and being transported to a hospital should be placed on a long spine board with a cervical collar to prevent secondary injury to the athlete. I have included step-by-step cervical spine board methods of transport in chapter 5.

If the athlete is unconscious, a clear airway is of utmost importance and should be firmly established and maintained throughout the spine boarding process. When the paramedics arrive, emergency intubation may be required if a clear airway cannot be obtained. Oxygen is typically administered to the athlete. Hemodynamic monitoring is needed to ensure proper circulation. Athletes with a dilated pupil or posturing may require moderate hyperventilation. Depending on condition, the athlete may be transported by traditional or air ambulance to the closest trauma center.

When the athlete reaches the hospital, the treatment of choice for a hematoma, aneurysm, or AVM swelling of the brain may include a craniotomy, which is performed by a neurosurgeon. During a craniotomy, a bony opening is cut into the skull. Craniotomies are used for the following reasons for sports trauma:

*to insert a shunt into the ventricles of the brain to drain CSF (hydrocephalus)

*to drain a blood clot (stereotactic hematoma aspiration)

*to insert an endoscope to clip aneurysms

Skull base craniotomies can be used to remove aneurysms, AVMS, or treat the brain following a skull fracture or injury. Complications of craniotomy include stroke; seizures; swelling of the brain, which may require a second craniotomy; nerve damage, which can cause muscle paralysis or weakness; CSF leak, which may require repair; loss of mental function; and permanent brain damage with associated disabilities. The results of the craniotomy depend a great deal on the underlying condition being treated

This information is offered to give you a general idea of what to expect if emergency treatment is necessary. Treatment will vary depending on the athlete's condition and the capability of the health-care facility.

The decision to disqualify an individual from further participation on the day of the concussive episode should be based on the sideline evaluation, the symptoms the athlete is experiencing, the severity of the apparent symptoms, and the patient's history. The literature is clear: any episode involving loss of consciousness or persistent symptoms related to concussion (headache, dizziness, amnesia, and so on), regardless of how mild and transient, warrants disqualification for the remainder of that day's activities

A qualified physician should supervise the management of a concussion and determine the timing of return to play. The physician should determine if symptoms have resolved, if cognition has recovered, and if the athlete should be gradually returned to athletic participation.

Return-to-Play Protocol

1. Complete Rest: After signs/symptoms of head trauma have resolved, proceed to #2.

2. Light Conditioning: Walk or ride exercise bike. If no problems, proceed to step #3.

3. Jogging/Running/Coordination Drills/Ball-Handling Drills: If no problem, proceed to step #4.

4. Full Practice Session (Noncontact): If no problem, proceed to step #5.

5. Full-Contact Practice After Medical Clearance: Observe for any problems after return to full contact.

The athlete should progress to the next step only if asymptomatic at the current level. If signs/symptoms increase, the athlete should be reevaluated by his or her physician.

Chapter 4

Cervical Spine Injury: Types of Injury/Evaluation and Treatment/Return-to-Play Decisions

An injury to the neck can occur in contact sports. Common mechanisms of cervical spine injury include a hockey player being pushed head-first into the boards, a football player striking an opponent with the crown of his helmet, a youth soccer player jumping up to head the ball and hitting the opponent head to head, or a gymnast who loses focus and lands head-first on the beam during a difficult flipping maneuver. Because of the risk of neck injuries, it is necessary for sports health-care professionals to understand anatomy and management techniques and guidelines for decisions about return to participation after cervical spine injury.

Axial loading of excessive force to the cervical spine has been documented as the primary cause of most neck injuries. When the head is in a neutral position, the normal alignment of the spine is one of extension because of the lordotic—unnatural—curve. With the head in a neutral position or further extended, forces of contact can be partially dissipated by an athlete's well developed musculature of the neck. When the head is rotated to a chin-down position even as little as thirty degrees, the normal cervical lordosis is straightened Which means that the normal forward or "c" shape curve in the neck is diminished, and the forces of impact to the top of the head are transmitted directly to the cervical spine.

When a player in this position collides with another player (called "spearing"), the head is stopped while the trunk is still moving, and the cervical spine is crushed between the two. Therefore, athletes who use the top of their helmet to tackle, block, or strike opponents are at greatest risk of cervical injury. Although using the helmet as an offensive battering ram must be discouraged, it is likely most of these dangerous maneuvers are not from intentional spearing or butt-blocking but from sloppy, poorly executed tackles and blocks. The athlete must overcome a natural tendency to tuck one's head when about to collide with an opponent. If this improper and harmful technique is disallowed by coaches of youth teams, the habit would be easier to break by the time an athlete reaches high school, where the majority of the serious spine injuries occur.

There are many types of injuries to the cervical region, including soft tissue injuries, skeletal injuries, and neurological injuries. Soft tissue injuries include muscle, tendon, and ligament injuries, which are the most common types of cervical injury. Athletes are more susceptible to muscular injury when they are fatigued. Whenever there is muscular spasm after a head-on collision or blow to the head or neck, a cervical spinal injury should be considered, especially when coupled with a decrease in cervical range of motion. A ligament injury may lead to instability of the cervical region.

Skeletal injuries include fractures of the cervical spine (Jefferson fracture of the ring of atlas/C1, flexion rotation fracture dislocation of the mid-cervical spine, vertebral body fracture, intervertebral facet fracture), cervical disk herniation, rupture of the atlantoaxial ligament, a main stabilizing ligament in the upper neck, anterior subluxation injury that involves a rupture of the posterior longitudinal ligament, and ligamentum flavum

Neurological injury to the cervical spine may include trauma involving the spinal cord, nerve root/spinal nerve complex, and brachial plexus. The most common cervical injury in football is the transient loss of function with radiating pain down one arm following a collision, commonly known as a "stinger." A stinger is a peripheral nerve injury, not a spinal cord injury. Initially, the athlete complains of total arm weakness and a radiating burning sensation that usually resolves within two to ten minutes. Numbness in the C6 dermatome may persist, along with motor weakness of shoulder abductors, elbow flexors, external humeral rotators, and wrist and finger extensors. The Spurling's Test may be positive. Stingers are thought to be the result of either a stretch injury, in which the head is driven to the side opposite the painful arm and the ipsilateral shoulder (shoulder on the same side of pain) is depressed, or the extended cervical spine is compressed and rotated toward the painful arm. Injury occurs because the cervical nerves are tethered by fibrous tissue between the vertebral arteries and the distal foramina at each cervical level. These dentate ligament attachments tighten and stretch the cervical nerve roots as they leave the spine. The key assessment of athletes with stingers is that the athlete should have full, pain-free, cervical ROM and normal motor and sensory testing before returning to play. Sideline examination must rule out any instability.

Other neurological conditions include disk herniation of the cervical region. An MRI or a CT is necessary to confirm diagnosis of this condition. Transient quadriplegia is a temporary paralysis that is characterized by a loss of motor or sensory function or both This is caused by a contusion of the spinal cord that produces a temporary restriction of blood flow to a portion of the cervical cord.

Evaluation and Treatment of Cervical Injury

Evaluation of cervical injury begins at the time of injury. It is imperative to know common signs and symptoms of a cervical fracture, which include the following:

*Pain in one part of the neck: Palpate for any deformity, swelling, or muscular spasm without moving the athlete's neck.

*Loss of feeling or pinprick pain in the athlete's arms or legs: Touch athlete on the arms, legs, and face, and ask him or her to tell you where you are touching; do this without moving the athlete.

*Muscle weakness or paralysis of the athlete's arms or legs: Ask athlete to grip your hand on each side and to push his or her foot gently against your hand; do this without moving the athlete.

*Pain radiating to athlete's shoulder or arm: Ask where the pain comes from and to where it radiates.

*Inability to move the neck or pain with movement of the athlete's neck: If the athlete says he or she cannot move the neck or that it is painful to move it, do not try to move the athlete's neck.

*Immediate bruising and/or swelling on the back of the neck may indicate injury.

If the athlete has any of the above signs or any signs/symptoms of cervical instability, he or she should be referred for examination by X-ray/ CT scan. You should always suspect and perform an evaluation for head trauma when a cervical spine injury is suspected. Plain film X-rays are taken to check normal alignment of the cervical vertebrae and active flexion-extension films are taken to determine ligamentous disruption during motion. CT scans and MRIs can view other structures of the cervical spine.

With the use of these diagnostic tools, cervical injuries can be classified according to injury level and area of fracture of the cervical vertebrae. Treatment may consist of surgical intervention for certain fractures, cervical immobilization, and the wearing of cervical collar or brace for less serious fractures or severe strain/sprains. Chiropractic manipulation can be very beneficial in the treatment of cervical segmental dysfunction or facet syndrome after a fracture has been ruled out. Physical therapy is beneficial in stabilizing and strengthening the injured structures of the neck.

Certain conditions may predispose the athlete to injury of the cervical spine. The most common abnormality is congenital stenosis, where the spinal canal is too small for the spinal cord. With spinal stenosis, the athlete may be more likely to have an episode of transient quadriplegia, stingers, to require surgery after a cervical disk herniation, run the risk of potential paralysis without a fracture/dislocation, or develop paralysis and a greater degree of paralysis after a fracture/dislocation

Klippel-Feil Syndrome is a congenital abnormality that involves fusion of segments of the cervical spine to produce hypermobility or instability in other areas of the neck. These conditions should be asked during the pre-participation exam and noted on the athlete's emergency medical card.

Conditions leading to a slightly increased risk of re-injury following initial cervical injury include asymptomatic bone spurs, healed non displaced fractures, stingers/burners, healed disk herniations, asymptomatic foraminal stenosis, and healed lamina fractures. Moderate risk conditions associated with significant chance for recurrence of symptoms and an increased risk for permanent injury include facet fracture; lateral mass fractures; acute lateral disk herniation; non displaced, healed odontoid fractures; and cervical radiculopathy secondary to foraminal spur. Extreme risk conditions with the highest risk of recurrence and of permanent damage include ruptured transverse ligament of C1–C2, occipitocervical dislocation, unstable fracture dislocations, cervical cord anomalies, acute cervical disk herniation, and osodontoideum.

Interview with Former NFL Football Player Mike Bartrum Whom sustained a cervical injury playing in the NFL

1. *Please describe your position and describe your NFL history?*

   I played thirteen NFL seasons: one for the Chiefs, one for the Packers, four for the Patriots, and seven years for the Eagles. I have two championship rings (Patriots and Eagles)—lost both Super Bowls—and played in one Pro Bowl. I played tight end and was a long snapper for punts and field goals.

2. *Please describe your injury to your neck.*

   I injured my neck on a tackle in 2006. I remember a pain/tingling going down my spine and both arms upon impact. The effect stayed for approximately five minutes, and I continued to play. After the game, my pain and stiffness continued to get worse. That was my last game in the NFL (November 2006). I had a disk herniation in my neck C3–4 with bulging disks at C5–6, with stenosis and compression.

3. *What initial treatment was provided to you at the time of injury?*

   An MRI was performed, which revealed my disk herniation, and the doctor put me in a neck collar. He gave me the option of surgery through the front of my neck or no surgery with rehab (traction, muscle stim, manual therapy, etc.). I opted for no surgery and retired while I could still walk and talk.

4. *Has your injury causd you ongoing problems?*
Yes. My neck has gotten worse since the injury, but I am trying everything I can to stay healthy and stay away from surgery.

5. *Did you sustain any diagnosed concussions while playing in the NFL?*
Yes. I sustained over five diagnosed concussions while playing in the NFL.

6. *Did you ever have signs/symptoms of a concussion that were not officially diagnosed while playing in the NFL (headache, dizziness, ringing in the ears, confusion, short-term memory loss, excessive fatigue, forgetfulness, imbalance, and so on)? If so, how many undiagnosed concussions would you suspect you sustained?*
Yes. Approximately twenty undiagnosed concussions.

7. *What signs/symptoms did you have if you answered yes to question 6?*

   My peripheral vision was the first to go (saw stars and everything went black) and then dizziness and headaches. I took it upon myself not to tell because of pressure and to not lose my job (playing time).

8. *While in the NFL, were you aware of any athletes who tried to downplay or hide their symptoms of a head/neck injury in order to continue playing?*

   Yes.

9. *Did your teammates take signs/symptoms of a concussion seriously or just blow it off as part of the profession?*

   They hid the injuries because of the pressure and fear of losing their job.

10. *What suggestions do you have for athletes regarding prevention of head-/neck-related injuries?*

    Football is a collision sport, and unless we get NASA involved with the structure of helmets, we are always going to have concussions because of the force, speed, intensity, etc., of football. The players are getting stronger, bigger, and faster every year!

CHAPTER 5

HOW TO CARE FOR AN ATHLETE WITH HEAD/NECK TRAUMA ON THE FIELD

After an injury, on field care is extremely important, so that the athlete gets the prompt attention he or she needs and to prevent further injury. If there is a neck injury, always expect a head injury, and if the athlete has sustained a concussion, always evaluate the neck as well.

For an Unconscious Athlete

1. Observe the level of consciousness. Evaluate the athlete's airway, breathing, and circulation. Remove mouthpiece if the athlete is wearing one. Look for the chest to rise, palpate athlete's pulse, listen for sounds, air coming from the mouth and nose.

2. If unconscious, activate the EMS by calling 911. Send someone to meet the squad at the gate and have AED (Automated External Defibrillator) ready in case you need it.

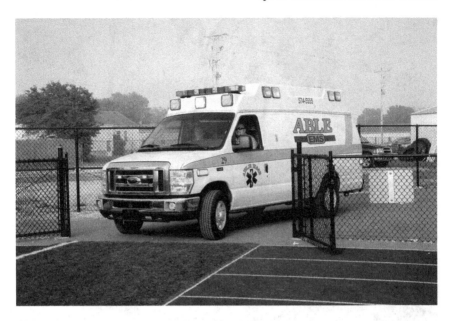

3. Stabilize the athlete's cervical spine with head/neck stabilization technique. (The medical team member at the head gives all commands.) If the athlete is facedown, make sure to cross your arms so that when you logroll the athlete, your hands will be in a comfortable position to give the best support to the athlete's cervical spine.

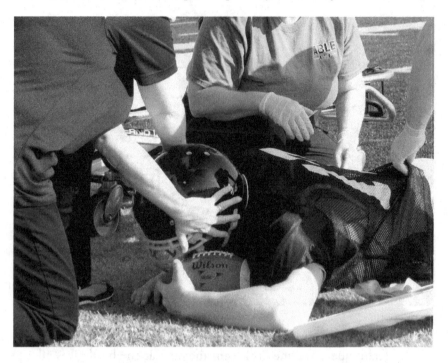

4. If the athlete is facedown, logroll onto his or her back and onto a spine board (if possible). If the athlete is vomiting, logroll the athlete to his or her side.

5. Cut the face mask clips or use an electric screwdriver to remove fasteners on the face mask for access. Record vitals every three to five minutes. Blood pressure and pulse can be taken by another health-care person while another removes the face mask from the helmet.

6. Place blocks around the head and fasten straps on spine board. Keep helmet on football players, and tape helmet down to spine board. Only remove the helmet if the face mask cannot be removed or flipped back and you need to sustain an airway (rescue breathing)

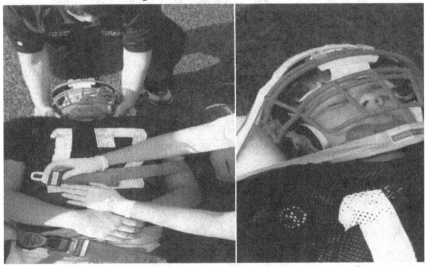

7. If needed, cut laces on shoulder pads to give access to chest.

8. Place the spine board on cot in unison with person stabilizing the athlete's neck giving verbal instructions, and transport athlete to EMS squad truck

9. Give the EMS the emergency card with vitals recorded and treatment performed before the squad arrived.

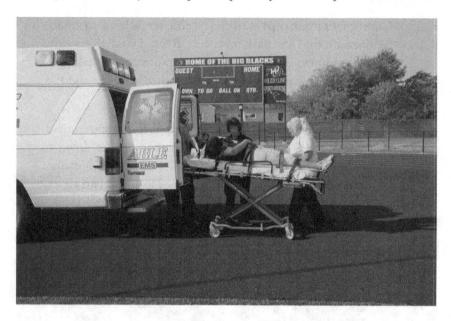

10. Once in the squad, the EMS may administer oxygen, insert an IV, and in life-threatening situations, may intubate the athlete.

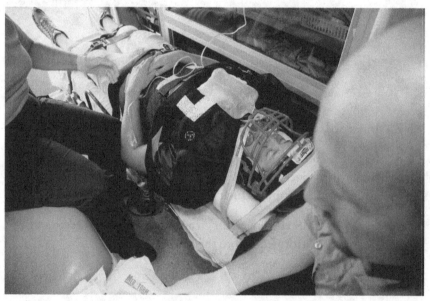

11. Make sure you give athlete's parent a head injury sheet and instructions on how to get to the ER.

When the athlete arrives at the ER, an X-ray should be taken of the athlete's neck while he or she is still strapped onto the spine board. Once a fracture and spinal cord injury has been ruled out, the chin strap will be removed and the cheek pads popped out with tongue depressors. The helmet will be tilted forward slightly and removed.

The athlete will need to have someone directly supervise him or her for the next forty-eight hours to make sure the situation does not deteriorate.

For the Athlete Having Neck Pain/Numbness or Tingling in Hands or Feet or Blacked Out

1. Observe level of consciousness. Check airway, breathing, circulation. Evaluate to determine if the athlete needs to be spine boarded.

2. Keep the athlete calm. Ask the athlete what happened. Tell the athlete to answer all questions verbally (not to shake or nod the head). Determine if athlete is aware of surroundings: Where are you at? What team are you playing? What is your jersey number? What team did you play last week?

3. Check athlete's pupil response to light.

4. Palpate the athlete's cervical spine to determine where pain is felt while observing and palpating for any signs of trauma, such as deformity, spasm, and edema.

5. Perform light touch sensory testing to all four extremities. Ask athlete to tell you where you are touching him or her.

6. To check grip strength, ask athlete to squeeze both of your hands.

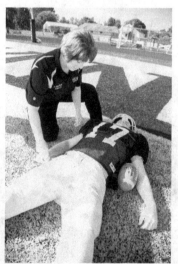

If the athlete has spinal pain, decreased sensory status, or motor deficit, do not perform the remainder of this exam. Place onto a spine board following the previous instructions and send to ER for further evaluation.

7. Ask the athlete to move his or her toes up and down.

8. Perform motor testing of upper and lower extremities.

9. Perform motor testing of upper and lower extremities.

   If the athlete has deficits on exam, transport. If exam is normal, gradually assist the athlete to a seated position while continuing to stabilize his or her neck. Ask if symptoms have changed after sitting up. Palpate the cervical spine while in a seated position. If no deformity, spinal pain, radiculopathy or tingling into extremities, assist the athlete to a standing position, observing for any changes in condition. Move to the sideline for further evaluation, observing for any sign the athlete is dizzy, unsteady, or in pain.

Sideline Evaluation

1. Ask the athlete what happened, have him or her describe mechanism of injury, and check to see if the athlete is aware of surroundings: Where are you? Who are you playing? What

is the score of the game? Who is winning? Who did you play last week? What position do you play? Ask if he or she has any symptoms of a concussion (headache, blurred vision, dizziness, nausea, confusion, neck pain, tingling in the arms, and so on). If he or she has a headache, ask the athlete to rate the pain on a scale of 1–10 (10 being the highest pain level), so you can determine later if the headache is improving or getting worse.

2. Ask the athlete to remember three numbers and then have him or her repeat them to you in reverse order. Have the athlete recite the days of the week and the months of the year backward. Ask if he or she remembers the score of the game last week, who won the game, who did the athlete played last week?

3. Take blood pressure and pulse and record.

4. Check pupil responsiveness to light.

5. Perform cardinal fields of vision tests.

6. Perform Rhomberg's Test.

7. Perform finger to nose test.

8. Palpate cervical spine.

9. Ask the athlete about increased signs/symptoms of head injury (dizziness, headache, confusion).

10. Ask the athlete to do a tandem walk.

11. Ask the patient to walk. Monitor constantly for signs symptoms have increased, as the athlete may not tell you everything he or she is experiencing due to the desire to go back in the game.

12. Ask the athlete to jog forward and backward three to five times. Instruct the athlete to stop immediately if symptoms worsen.

13. Have the athlete do three squats, side-to-side shuffles, and ten push-ups.

14. Repeat exam items 1–6.

If any abnormalities are detected on the exam but the athlete is improving, reevaluate in three to five minutes while continuing to monitor the athlete constantly.

If the condition worsens, transport immediately. Parents can choose to take their child to the ER, but it is highly recommended the athlete be transported in a squad. The status of a head injury can change for the worse very quickly.

CHAPTER 6

PREVENTION OF HEAD/NECK TRAUMA

Concussions, cervical fractures, and spinal cord injuries cannot be totally eliminated from sports participation, but the risk of sustaining a catastrophic (life-ending) injury or paralysis can be greatly reduced. Proper fitting of sports equipment, awareness of the warning signs an athlete has a problem, and learning when it is safe to allow him or her to return to play can help reduce the likelihood of catastrophic injury. Teaching proper technique, conditioning, and neck strengthening techniques, and enforcing safety rules can also aid in the prevention of injury. The age and maturation of the athlete also plays a role in prevention. It is suggested that tackle football should not be played by children under ten years old, and youth teams should be matched by skill and size ("Position Statement"). Because of the potential for harm from multiple lesser impacts to the head, the benefits of monitoring the number of blows to the head is being researched and considered. Dr. Cantu says, "It's necessary to take a page from another game—baseball. We have pitch counts for pitchers from Little League to the Majors, who want to limit the number of pitches they throw and protect their arms. We're probably going to have to go to hit counts to the head in our football players to protect the brain" (Goldman).

The pre-participation physical exam plays an important role in detecting conditions that could predispose an athlete to injury or illness during practice or competition. The athlete should understand the basic rules of football related to injury prevention and should be able to demonstrate the fundamental athletic skills, particularly blocking and tackling without using the head, and should do these hitting drills repetitively while keeping the head up.

Conditioning programs should promote aerobic and anaerobic endurance, flexibility, range of motion, and power and strength training. If an athlete is tired during competition, proper execution of technique is greatly reduced and places the athlete at an increased risk for injury. To reduce the risk of spinal injury, athletes should perform specific shoulder, upper back, and neck flexibility and strengthening exercises, so the athlete will be able to hold his or her head up firmly during blocking and tackling in football and other sporting events.

Wearing the proper sports equipment and checking to make sure it is fitted properly are extremely important in the prevention of head/neck trauma. Each athlete should have the safest available equipment. Helmets should meet safety standards set by the National Operating Committee on Standards in Athletic Equipment (NOCSAE). They should be checked for cracks in the shell; loose screws, rivets, or other fasteners; compromised pads; holes or cracks in fluid or air compartments; and distorted face masks ("Position Statement"). Sharp edges, scratch marks, or deep paint marks from previous games can increase friction on the surface of the helmet and contribute to greater force against the head during impact. Rusted or stripped screws need to be replaced, and old or damaged equipment should be properly reconditioned by a professional or thrown away.

The work of developing a football helmet standard began in 1970. A test system was designed to decrease the likelihood of athletes sustaining traumatic head/neck trauma. The equipment was designed for the initial certification tests, installed in manufacturing plants, and manufacturers assumed responsibility for certification. In a pioneering effort by one of the largest helmet reconditioners, installation of a device which tests forces which helmets take when taking hits from various angles, in 1975 found that 84 percent of the used helmets failed the NOCSAE test. The National Athletic Equipment Reconditioner's Association (NAERA) became a member of NOCSAE in 1976, and they revised the NOCSAE football helmet standard in 1977, requiring recertification of helmets by reconditioners. The NCAA mandated the use of certified helmets in 1978, and the National Federation of State High School Associations required them from the beginning of the 1980 season. These changes resulted in a decrease in the death rate from head and neck injuries in football (*National Operating*). These regulations were not the sole reduction factor in football-related fatalities, since warning and enforcement against spearing and other rule changes have also played a role in the decrease of football-related fatalities.

Helmets should be fitted by a knowledgeable, experienced person. During helmet fitting, hair should be at normal length and should be wet to best simulate the actual condition of the hair during competition. If an athlete shaves his head after helmet fitting, the helmet needs to be refitted. An athlete with an irregular head shape may get a more effective fit with an air helmet, because this type of helmet better conforms to the head.

Players need to be instructed on how to put on the helmet properly. They should place two thumbs in earholes, with the helmet tilted back, and then roll the helmet forward onto the head. The front edge of the helmet should rest approximately three-fourths of an inch above the eyebrow. The athlete's ear and helmet earhole should match up. There should be three-fourths to no more than one and one-half inches of space between the athlete's head and the outer shell of the helmet. The back of the helmet should not impinge on the cervical spine when the neck is extended.

To test the fit, the jaw pads should be removed, and the athlete should flex his neck, resisting the fitter's efforts to rotate the helmet from side to side. If the skin on the forehead does not move with the helmet, the helmet is not snug enough. The helmet should also be rotated up and down to be sure the front edge of the shell does not come down on the bridge of the athlete's nose. Jaw pads of proper thickness will help minimize side-to-side rotation of the helmet. There should be no space between the jaw pads and the jaw and cheek. A four-point chin strap is suggested, with equal tension on all four attachments and no slack in the straps. The chin strap should be centered on the chin. The face mask opening should be small enough to keep out forearms and shoes. If the bar is fitted too low, it doesn't protect the facial area sufficiently. If it is fitted too high, it obstructs vision and exposes the mandible to injury. The space between the top edge of the shell's face opening and the top bar of the face mask should not exceed three inches. The mask should be attached with plastic straps that help absorb shock when a blow is delivered to the face. Plastic or rubber straps also make it possible to remove the face mask in the event of an emergency. The amount of air that gives the helmet the additional compression needed to keep the helmet snug on the head is measured and should be recorded. Variations in weather (hot vs. cold) may affect the amount of air needed in the helmet.

After proper fitting, mark the helmet with the athlete's name and jersey number. The helmet should be worn only by that individual athlete.

Periodic refitting may be necessary due to haircuts, compression of pads, or loss of air from compartments. I suggest refitting of the helmet by a professional if an athlete sustains a Grade II or Grade III concussion before returning to play.

For youth football, the University of Pittsburgh conducted a three-year study of over two thousand high school football players. The results showed that the Riddell Revolution helmet provides better protection than traditional helmets. Athletes wearing the Revolution were 31 percent less likely to suffer a concussion than if wearing a traditional helmet, and 41 perent less likely to sustain a concussion if they had never experienced a concussion before ("Revolution Helmet").

Athletes experience repeated impacts when tackling and being tackled. These often lead to minor concussions that can go unnoticed. Due to the macho nature of football, athletes often continue playing after incurring an injury, increasing the risk of sustaining further brain damage. As a sports medicine practitioner, it is often difficult to determine when an athlete may have sustained a concussion, and we have given feedback to helmet designers to see if there is a way to test the amount of impact to determine if the athlete sustained trauma to the brain. Riddell has developed a helmet that measures the location, direction, and severity of an impact. The Revolution Hits IQ is equipped with six accelerometers located within the helmet lining. The sensors, which are the same as those used in airbags, measure the linear and rotational acceleration of the head that occurs following a powerful impact. The impact data is transmitted wirelessly to a laptop computer with software that translates it into a reaction force ("New Football"). Riddell already supplies similar impact-detecting helmets to a number of university football teams in the United States, and individual helmets are now available. The helmet comes with a response system that sends an alert to the trainer when a player experiences an impact above a predetermined threshold. Simbex is testing the same technology in soccer headbands and in hockey and skiing helmets. Simbex has also developed combat helmets for the US Army equipped with the new technology.

The difficulty has been to detect at what threshold an athlete actually sustains a concussion, as some athletes demonstrate no signs/symptoms of a concussion when the response mechanism showed a high impact. Duma and associates were the first to use acceleration-measuring technology in helmets for large numbers of athletes during normal practice and game situations. His group used the Head Impact Technology (HIT) System technology (Simbex, Lebanon, New Hampshire) incorporated within the Sideline Response System (Riddell Corp., Elyria, Ohio). The HIT system is composed of six spring-loaded, single-axis accelerometers that are inserted into football helmets. Research is currently being done on impact biomechanics, hoping to determine proposed injury thresholds. This research may help us to understand why some athletes are able to withstand very high magnitude impacts without much deficit, whereas others show deficits (signs/symptoms of concussion) with significantly lower magnitude impacts.

Helmet companies are constantly looking for a new helmet design to safely protect the skull and brain. They have changed the size, shape, and weight, added more padding, used air, and so on in attempts to provide safer protection. Riddell's closest rival, Schutt Sports, hasn't changed its basic helmet shape in the past fifteen years. Schutt released a new, lighter helmet, the Air Advantage, with slightly different features and has field-tested a prototype with more padding.

Football helmet manufacturers face a unique challenge. Motorcycle and race-car helmets are made to be discarded after one severe impact, but football and hockey helmets must be soft enough to cushion routine hits, sturdy enough to absorb the force of violent helmet-to-helmet collisions, and durable enough to withstand the hits week after week.

In the early 1900s, the first helmets were made of leather. Manufacturers developed a stiff polycarbonate shell lined with dense foam padding to protect the athlete from skull fracture and subdural hematomas, and those types of injuries have reduced.

The major challenge is preventing the brain trauma caused by repetitive, less-intense collisions. Xenith has replaced the traditional foam with a "shock bonnet": an adjustable cap housing eighteen plastic shock absorbers, shaped like small hockey pucks, each of them hollow with a tiny hole on top. The concept is that when an athlete takes or gives a relatively mild hit, the pressure forces air out of the pinholes, dispelling force by deflating the absorber until it is flat as a saucer. When the pressure is removed, the absorber re-inflates quickly, and the helmet is ready for the next impact (Starkey).

Another challenging problem manufacturers face is the rattling of a player's brain inside the skull, often caused by rotational force. When an athlete experiences a rotational mechanism, the theory is that the rotation of the cerebrum about the brain stem produces shearing and tensile strains. Rotational mechanisms of traumatic brain injury (concussion) are believed to be more likely to result in loss of consciousness in an athlete than the linear types of impacts, mainly because the activities in the midbrain and upper brain stem are responsible for alertness and responsiveness (Ommaya and Gennarelli).

Mouth Guards

It has been known for years that mouth guards provide great protection from oral or facial injuries that occur in contact sports. They provide protection from fractured teeth and jaw fractures. A controversial topic today in sports medicine and biomechanics is whether mouth guards provide any protection against concussions.

There are three basic types of mouth guards. Stock mouth guards can be purchased anywhere and are the cheapest. But they often don't fit properly, so they probably don't provide that much protection. Boil and bite mouth guards are the most popular. They are immersed in boiling water and then molded to the athlete's mouth. If not molded properly, so the posterior teeth are covered, they don't provide much protection either. The third type of mouth guard is the custom-made mouth guard, where a dentist creates a mold of the athlete's mouth and then can properly fit it for the athlete.

A multitude of studies have been done looking at mouth guard materials and testing energy absorption properties of various materials. They provide better insight into how mouth guards may help prevent concussions. The elasticity of the material determines how much impact energy it will absorb, thereby determining the effectiveness of the mouth guard. If the elastic limit is exceeded, permanent deformation occurs, making the mouth guard less effective. The most common used material used in making mouth guards is ethylene vinyl acetate (EVA).

Upper-only mouth guards allow the lower jaw to move freely and cannot stabilize the jaw, therefore putting the athlete at risk of jaw-joint injury and concussion. . The bones of the jaw complex contain the cranial nerve trunks as they exit the brain. They also contain the main blood supply to the brain and the hearing and balance mechanisms, among others (McMaster University).

Bimolar mouth guards are promising new technology, in which the upper and lower teeth are covered by the mouth guard. It is suggested that this new design allows for increased protection from concussion due to blows to the mandible (lower jaw), which can cause impact to the base of the skull at the temporomandibular joint (TMJ) and lead to a concussion. Bimolar mouth guards are primarily manufactured by Brain-Pad. They have developed a dual arch technology that gives athletes a breathing space at the front of the guard. Wayne State University tested the quality and protection of the Brain-Pad mouth guards using head-form drop test procedures. They found that the Brain-Pad mouth guard holds the lower jaw forward and down, so there is no sliding. The safety space is better maintained during impact compared to the regular boil and bite or custom-made mouth guards (Brain-Pad).

Dr. V. R. Hodgson, director of the NOCSAE, and the Biomechanics Research Center at Wayne State University were in charge of the studies conducted involving the Brain-Pad mouth guard. The university conducted the studies using an articulated epoxy head form drop test: the head form was tested to be mechanically similar to a cadaver head. An accelerometer and several forms of transducers were placed along the mandible, face, and jaw joint. The test was conducted using a sixty-inch drop height; a helmet with a chin cup was used to mimic football helmet impact to the face mask and the forces delivered to the base of the skull. Another test was performed with a helmet and from a drop of six inches. It was shown that Brain-Pad mouth guards disperse the forces more evenly over the surface of the mouth guard to lessen the severity of the impact, and they reduce the peak force by half compared to styles of mouth guards. The total forces transmitted were also found to be reduced by as much as 40 percent when wearing Brain-Pad, when compared to not wearing it (Brain-Pad).

Boxers have known for years that the easiest way to knock out their opponent is to throw a blow to his jaw, because an impact to the lower jaw drives the jaw bone up into the TMJ area and base of the skull. Studies have proven that over 90 percent of concussions resulting in unconsciousness are from impacts to the jaw (McMaster University). As a team physician, I have seen a tremendous reduction in the incidence of concussions in the teams who wear only the Brain-Pad mouth guards, compared to the teams whose athletes still use the thin, upper -molar only mouth guards over the past several years.

Everyone Plays a Role in the Prevention of Head/Neck Trauma

Everyone has a role in the prevention of injury for an athlete. Following is a list of a few of the responsibilities of those involved with athletes in the prevention of head/neck injury.

The Coach's Role in Prevention of Head/Neck Trauma

The coach has several responsibilities for the safety of the athletes. It is his or her responsibility to teach safety principles and proper techniques— and to reinforce that proper technique during practice sessions. For example, in football, players need to be taught the helmet is a protective device, not a weapon, as the head should not be used as a battering ram when blocking or tackling. Contact needs to be made with the head up and never with the top of the head/helmet. Initial contact should never be made with head/helmet or face mask.

One study on injury biomechanics in American football players, conducted at the University of North Carolina, uses a real-time helmet accelerometer data collection methodology in Division I college players. Their findings suggest a higher relative risk of concussion for top of the head impacts. In this regard, six of thirteen concussions occurred from impacts to the top of the head. The findings also suggest top of the helmet impacts may result in larger postural stability deficits after traumatic brain injury (concussion; Guskiewicz, Mihalik, Shankar et al.). It was suggested that top of the helmet impacts result in a coup-contrecoup mechanism occurring by taking a blow to the top of the helmet which transmits the force downward , causing the cerebellum to impact the base of the skull and recoil superiorly into the cerebellar tentorium. These impacts to the top of the head are also at least six times more likely to result in impact magnitudes greater than 80g of linear acceleration than side or front impacts (Mihalik, Bell, Marshall, and Guskiewicz). Technique is important in all sports, not just football. Proper heading of the ball in soccer needs to be taught and practiced, proper sliding into the base in baseball/softball, proper landing technique in gymnastics/tumbling, and so on.

It is also the coach's job to make sure athletes are properly conditioned. Coaches are also responsible for making sure the environment is safe for the athletes: posts are padded and dangerous weather is monitored, so athletes do not compete where and when they might be more prone to hit head to head. Coaches must not push the athletes beyond their physical capability. Coaches need to be aware of the signs/symptoms of head/neck trauma and to make sure any injured athlete gets evaluated by medical professionals if he or she shows any signs/ symptoms of a head/ neck problem in practice sessions, at school, or in a game. Coaches need to stay updated on emergency procedures and obtain the appropriate injury prevention and safety training, and they must make sure the equipment is properly fitted and maintained for each athlete.

The Team Physician's Role in Prevention of Head/Neck Injury

The role of the team physician begins with the pre-participation sports physical. The physician should take a complete history of prior neck trauma, inquire about any congenital abnormalities, and ask questions about any previous concussions or signs/symptoms of concussion. Then, the team physician should make a list of those with a history of any of these problems and make sure those athletes in particular are watched closely for any signs/symptoms of concussion. The team physician should also implement an emergency medical plan for his or her particular team, which would include knowing the emergency phone contacts, where the squad is at each game, and practicing spine board techniques prior to the season. The team physician may have the team take a preseason cognitive test as a baseline for concussions and present an educational session to athletes and parents prior to the season.

The team physician is responsible for evaluating any athletes suspected of a head/neck injury, making return-to-play decisions, and for providing the on-field care of that athlete. In short, the team physician is responsible for doing everything possible to provide a safe environment for the athlete.

The Trainer's Role in Prevention of Head/Neck Injury

The certified athletic trainer should develop an injury prevention program. He or she should also create a medical emergency plan and practice it with the coaching staff prior to the beginning of the season. It is the certified athletic trainer's responsibility to evaluate injuries and contact EMS or send the athlete to the appropriate sports physician for evaluation following a head/neck injury. Another important role of the Certified Athletic Ttrainer is to communicate with the team physician on a regular basis, updating him or her on injured athletes. It is the trainer's responsibility to observe carefully any athletes during practice sessions after they have been released to play following a concussion. The trainer must report any abnormalities to the team physician. It is the responsibility of the trainer to obtain a report of any activity restrictions placed on the athletes and to make sure they are followed by the athlete and coach. It is the trainer's role to observe athletes for any abnormalities in behavior and any signs/symptoms of head/neck trauma. It is the trainer's responsibility to remove the athlete from participation until thoroughly evaluated by the team physician.

Trainers must also monitor the sports equipment and make sure it is properly fit for the athletes. The trainer also plays a role in making sure the environment is safe for the athletes (poles are padded, and so on).

The trainer is required to contact the athlete's parents (if under eighteen years of age) and give the parent a head injury sheet of signs/symptoms to watch for twenty-four to forty-eight hours posttraumatic brain injury, even if it appears to be a "possible" concussion, as head injuries can progressively get worse, and signs/symptoms may not always show up immediately.

The Parents' Role in Prevention of Head/Neck Trauma

Parents need to be educated about the inherent risks of trauma to the head/neck with contact sports and preventative measures to decrease the likelihood of head/neck trauma. They need to report any injury that occurs at home or in athletics to the sports medicine staff. Parents need to reinforce to their child the importance of complying with any restrictions on participation recommended by the sports health-care team. Parents also need to be aware of the signs/symptoms of a concussion and report any of those findings to the health-care team. They need to observe their child closely for twenty-four to seventy-two hours post concussion and follow the head injury sheet given to them by the health-care professional. Parents should *never* give their child aspirin or aspirin-containing products while participating in sports, because aspirin thins the blood and increases the risk of a brain bleed when a head trauma occurs.

The Role of Officials in the Prevention of Head/Neck Trauma

Officials at sporting events should know the rules and enforce those rules strictly during athletic competition (especially spearing and late hits). Prior to the competition, they are required to evaluate the playing field for any potentially unsafe conditions. They should tell the coach or sports medicine team if they see an athlete who appears confused or dazed, or if an athlete is using incorrect technique that could potentially cause injury to himself or the opponent. Officials should stop play immediately if there is an injured athlete on the field and keep other athletes away from him or her to avoid further injury, possibly by incorrectly moving the athlete, for example.

The Role of the Athlete in Prevention of Head/Neck Trauma

The athlete is responsible for performing a conditioning and strength program prior to the season. He or she must master correct execution of athletic techniques and follow the rules of the game. The athlete is responsible for wearing proper protective equipment and not tampering with it (cut the mouthpiece, take air out of their helmet, and so on). Each athlete is responsible for reporting any injury to the health-care team immediately. All athletes must *be honest* about signs/symptoms of a head or neck problem. The athlete is responsible for complying with treatment protocols and for following the restrictions the health-care professional puts in place to prevent further injury.

Further Measures Which are Important in the Prevention of Head/Neck Trauma

Prevention of head/neck trauma is the primary concern for the sports medicine professional, parents, and coach. There are three Es that I feel are important regarding prevention of head/neck trauma for our current and future generations.

Education

We must educate athletes, parents, and coaches about head and neck injuries and help them to learn the signs/symptoms of a concussion, the importance of doing drills properly, and the importance of being honest about injuries. They must also learn the importance of complying with restrictions placed on athletic participation when necessary.

Enforcement

We must make sure that sports-specific rules are enforced and a mechanism for punishment put in place if not followed. All involved in sports (coaches, officials, athletes, parents, and sports medicine professionals) must stay updated on rule changes.

Engineering

We must continue to do more research and constantly seek the most protective sports equipment possible. Head injuries are the most common direct cause of death among football players. Athletes who use the head to make contact dramatically increase their risk of sustaining serious injury. However, there has been a dramatic decrease in brain injury–related fatalities since the late 1960s, and research has concluded helmet design and establishment of safety standards by the NOCSAE are largely responsible for this decline ("Preventing").

The Role of Rule Changes/Regulations in Prevention of Head/Neck Trauma

Cheerleading, with approximately two direct catastrophic injuries per year, is the number-one sport responsible for female direct catastrophic injuries. It accounts for more than half of the catastrophic injuries in high school and collegiate female athletes ("Preventing").

Over the last couple of decades, cheerleading has evolved into a physically demanding sport, requiring complex gymnastic maneuvers that pose serious injury threats to participants. Due to the susceptibility of injury during pyramid formations, the National Federation of State High School Association and the NCAA have set limits on pyramid height—two levels in high school and two and one-half body lengths in college—and included specifications on spotters. Safety measures have also been put in place for the basket toss, limiting the stunt to four throwers, banning flips, and positioning one of the throwers behind the top person during the toss. Further recommendations include increased spotter training, limiting the number of cheerleaders involved in pyramids, mandating the use of floor mats for complex stunts, prohibiting stunts when surfaces are wet, restricting the height thrown for basket tosses, and requiring certification for coaches. These are all to prevent head/neck traumas in cheerleaders.

Research reveals that rule changes have contributed to the decline of catastrophic injury in other sports. Hockey has put in place rules prohibiting pushing or checking from behind and recommend full facial protection. In baseball, the NCAA and NFHS now require all high school and college bats to be labeled with a permanent certification mark that a ball exit speed cannot exceed a certain speed when tested on a standardized batting device. Limitations have also been placed on bat thickness and weight, and there is research looking at changing the hard shell of baseballs.

In soccer, the US Consumer Product Safety Commission cited twenty-one deaths over a sixteen-year period and they have implemented some changes which have helped to decrease the number of deaths by initiating some basic rules and safety standards:prevention mechanisms to keep goalposts from tipping and never allowing children to play or swing on goalposts ("Preventing").

The Zides family has been working diligently with sports equipment safety for over fifty years. They have been fitting football equipment for local high schools and colleges and have performed some studies on helmets and even have several patents on helmet and mouthguard designs.

Interview with Rodney Zide, President of Zides Sport Shop of Ohio, Inc., and President of Proline, Inc.

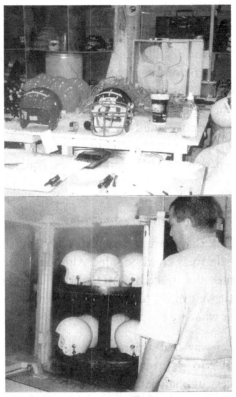

1. *The Zides family has been fitting helmets for decades. Can you tell me a little about your company and how it got started, and explain what you do at Zides Sports Shop?*

   My father, Bob Zide, started the company in 1958 with the idea of making athletics as safe as possible. In sports, equipment is the key. Players from pee-wee to the pros rely on proven products for safety, performance, and a competitive edge. Zides is the sports equipment leader in tradition, innovation, and performance. Nine product patents, an extensive inventory, the largest and most modern lettering factory in that area, and a sales team with over two hundred years of experience all help form the best equipment team in the industry.

2. *What can I do as a parent to protect my child from concussion?*

   I don't think that there is parent in the world that does not want to help their child be safer. Although there is no way to guarantee that tragedy won't ever strike, there are some things that we can do to hopefully decrease the likelihood, and that is what we try to do.

   An indirect way that a parent can help protect their child from injury is to get involved and help the program to become more successful financially, which will, in turn, help the kids become better equipped. Parents need to make sure that their child maintains their equipment. You need to look at it, make sure that the screws are tight, that the bladder is inflated properly, that the parts are in the helmet properly, the Velcro hasn't come loose, and that the face mask isn't bent. A bent face mask distorts the way the helmet fits on the head and, therefore, changes the way the helmet is fit on the player. A properly fit helmet is much more protective, because it allows the helmet to do its job better.

   You need to make sure that your child has a good mouth guard and a hard-cup chin strap that is fastened properly. A chin strap is just like a seat belt: if you don't wear it properly, it's not going to help you as much as if you wear it properly.

3. *What piece of equipment is the most important in protecting athletes from concussion?*

Obviously, the helmet plays an important role in protection from skull injuries and head trauma, but there are many variables with a helmet. You can take an old football helmet or a traditional-shaped helmet and make that helmet more protective by fitting it properly, but a new helmet offers the best protection, because it has less fatigue placed on it than the older helmet. There are helmets which have more padding on the inside, more standoff; they call them large offset helmets, which means they have an inch-thick pad all the way around the head, theoretically they have a half inch or one and three-quarter inches.

Running a close second, or maybe all tied for first, is a properly fit, hard, low-cup chin strap and a properly fitted, bimolar, thick mouth guard.

4. *How does a mouth guard help reduce the risk of sustaining a concussion?*

From what I have seen, been told, and read about, your body has some natural ability to absorb energy to your bones and your joints, or through your tissue. In your teeth, you don't have quite that forgiveness. Anything that happens in your jaw and your upper and lower palate, because it is so close to the brain, gets to the brain quicker. Obviously, what you are trying to do in any type of collision is to absorb energy and reduce the force going to the athlete's brain. A mouth guard can absorb the energy coming in through the jaw before it gets to the brain. I highly recommend an upper and lower palate mouth guard, trague mouth guard, something that actually helps align the lower jaw better. Kids are going to grit their teeth when they have impacts. That is just part of the process, so you want something between the teeth to absorb that energy.

5. *In your opinion, which mouth guard provides the best protection against concussion and Why?*

I am only speaking from our experience, as we have tried to sell a variety of different styles of mouth guards. In my opinion, we have had great success with the Brain-Pad, particularly the Pro Plus mouth guard. The Brain-Pad is thicker, probably the thickest guard that I have seen. It has an upper and lower tray, and it has air openings, which allow the athlete to breathe better with the teeth clenched. This mouth guard also uses a variety of materials, because one material cannot do two different jobs. Mouth guard material is usually hard and designed for severe impacts or soft and designed for softer impacts.

Then, just like a pair of shoes, mouth guards wear out. Most kids only get one mouth guard and think it will last them through an entire athletic season, but the kids chew on them, decreasing their protective ability. An athlete typically needs to utilize two to three mouth guards to maintain the most protection during a season.

6. *Which football helmet do you feel provides the most protection against concussion in football, and why?*

This is a tough question because each company performs tests which try to make their particular helmet look better. I think, in fairness, that we probably—as an industry—need to look at how we are testing for a football helmet and come up with a set of standards that look at concussions and tests for concussions a little differently. Most of the helmet testing now is basically looking at skull fractures and not designed to take concussion into account.

My personal opinion is the best helmet is a brand new helmet. I prefer a larger offset helmet. A DNA, Speed, a Schutt DNA, a Riddell, Zenith X1: those helmets are all larger offset helmets. They are designed with more padding on the inside, so they will absorb more energy.

It is really hard to say which helmet protects against concussion the best, because there are so many variables. It depends on the temperature, the humidity, the fit of the helmet on that particular athlete, etc. Personally, we sell the Schutt DNA, because I like the way it fits. This helmet has a material on the inside of the helmet that is not affected by temperature and is not affected as much by moisture when compared to other brands.

The biggest problem with air helmets is that they require a lot of maintenance, and most athletes do not maintain their helmet as they should. We try to fit every helmet that we sell and recondition, and have found the DNA, which is a larger offset helmet, to be one of the better helmets.

7. *Does thick hair interfere with the way a helmet fits, thus decreasing the amount of protection that the helmet provides?*

Players with a lot of hair will often pull it all to the back, and that makes the back of the helmet want to sit up, which puts the helmet in an improper position. When we are fitting a player, their hair is typically dry, but when playing, the head is wet from sweat, so on occasion, we will actually have an athlete wet their hair, so we can actually see how it is going to fit on the field. Hair is a tough variable. It definitely affects how the helmet fits. And again, if the helmet is not fitting right, it will be less protective.

8. *What suggestions do you have for coaches to help in prevention of head/neck injuries?*

I think coaches have come a long way in teaching the players to keep their heads up and look at what they are hitting, but coaches still need to remind and teach proper hitting/tackling techniques and need to make sure that the athletes are strengthening their necks. For a head injury, the key is newer equipment, not trying to get ten years out of your football helmets. Football helmets go through a lot of contact. I think the average helmet gets somewhere in the area of sixteen hundred hits/year. If you do that over a period of ten years, you are talking about sixteen thousand hits. I don't think there is a car or anything that can take sixteen thousand impacts. So obviously, you want to rotate your equipment and keep newer equipment on the field, especially helmets and shoulder pads.

Everyone wants to get the best-looking jerseys and pants, and that's great—look good—but the most important thing to do is to make sure that those kids are in good helmets and shoulder pads. They also need a good mouth guard and chin strap, and the helmets need to be reconditioned every year. You want to make sure that reconditioning includes taking the helmet apart and inspecting the inside pads individually. Reconditioning should be more than just washing and repainting the helmet to make it look good. Before we send a helmet back to the school, every part is personally hand inspected.

9. *What suggestions do you have for athletes to help prevent head/ neck injury?*

    Make sure that everything fits properly and that everything is working, your helmet bladders don't have holes in them, your helmet obviously doesn't have a crack, and the face mask should not be bent.

    To prevent neck injury, make sure that you properly strengthen the neck and practice proper tackling/blocking technique. I cannot emphasize enough to *keep the head up!* A lot of kids try to lead with their heads. If you look at Division I college football players, their helmets aren't torn up at all. Or if you look at the pros, their helmets aren't torn up. We get some high school helmets sent back for reconditioning, and you would be amazed at how torn up they are. It is obvious that these kids have been leading with their heads. You want to keep your head out of the contact and not use your helmet as a battering ram.

10. *Are younger children (under age twelve) more susceptible to head trauma?*

    A youth player is not as developed as a varsity player, but he is typically not being hit as hard either. The main problem with youth football is the equipment. Youth programs historically have a hard time financially, so they either buy the cheapest equipment on the market, or they use old equipment from the high school team. Many of the youth helmets on the market are scary when you look at how they are built and designed. There are certain youth helmets which we refuse to sell, because they can't be fit properly. A proper fitting helmet is always the best helmet.

The other problem with youth football is that the person running the program is typically a parent, and for the first year, this person isn't as knowledgeable on equipment as I would like them to be. By the time his kid is ready to move up to junior high, he is pretty knowledgeable, he knows how a helmet should fit, how to maintain the helmet, etc. Then, he moves on up the ladder with his son, and a new person takes over that again has no clue how to fit or maintain the equipment.

Another equipment problem in youth football is that they don't have the parts to maintain their equipment, and typically, their equipment is not reconditioned every year.

Research has shown that kids with concussions in the youth age are more likely to get repeat concussions as they age. These kids need to be taught how to fit their helmet, how to put the helmet on, how to wear the helmet, the importance of the mouth guard, how to fasten the chin strap, and how to hit properly.

11. *What new products are coming in the near future to help reduce the incidence of concussion?*

They are trying to tweak the helmet, the mouth guard, and the chin strap, always looking for a better, more protective product. Helmets are now being changed by manufacturers every two to three years, as they are trying to do everything they can to keep these kids safe. I don't know of any earth-shattering pieces of equipment that are coming out right now, but there is attention being drawn to the way the helmets are tested and the need to do more to test for concussion.

12. *What process does a helmet go through when reconditioned?*

The reconditioning of the helmet is supposed to include: taking the face mask off, visually inspecting the helmet, and testing is supposed to be done on 2 percent of the helmets which you recondition and then you test the helmets afterward.

We actually strip every one of our helmets, look at each pad separately, and then we try to set our level of testing at 10 percent. If we had a machine that would allow you to test them all, that would be the best. Testing a helmet is time consuming. If we could get a machine that would test faster, we would gladly do it. The key to reconditioning is that it should be more than just sanitizing it or placing the screws or nuts, or painting it and sending it back to the school. We have had pads come through our reconditioning plant where a player, I assume a player, has taken their front pad out and hollowed out the back of the pad to make it more comfortable. That is a scary situation. If you are not taking that helmet apart and catching that, you don't want to send that to someone else. There needs to be a higher standard of replacing the parts and an attempt to increase the testing percentage.

13. *During the season, how many times should equipment be checked by coaching staff? What needs to be checked?*

Assuming that you started out with a properly fit football helmet that was in good working condition, and all parts were intact, face mask was not bent, all screws and nuts were tight, the jaw pads fit snug, the air was recorded, and they were then given to the coach, the helmets should be checked weekly. You need to inspect the helmet inside as well as the shell. Make sure that the screws are not loose on the helmet, double-check the air in the helmet, and make sure that the jaw pads fit snugly against the athlete's cheeks. A sure sign that the face mask is bent is when the jaw pads are not firmly against the cheeks. You need to check the shell for cracks or deep grooves on the top of the helmet. Most of the time, a helmet will crack where it has been drilled from the face mask. Check that area. You want to make sure that the helmet is holding air. Then, put it back on the athlete, and make sure that the jaw pads fit snuggly against the cheeks.

14. *What are the most common problems with helmets popping off during football participation?*

Assuming we start out with a properly fit helmet, the single most important thing you can do to keep a helmet from popping off is to wear a low, hook-up, hard chin strap and have it fastened properly. A large majority of the players do not fasten their chin straps properly. In my opinion, it is almost impossible to fasten a high-cup chin strap properly. The front two snaps on the chin strap do most of the work. You need to make sure that the chin strap is even and tight.

15. *What can medical professionals do to help reduce the incidence of concussion?*

The medical professionals need to help educate the coaches and equipment managers as to what to look for in the helmet. Are the helmets properly fit? Have the helmets been maintained? Are the athletes wearing the large, offset helmets? Do the athletes have a good mouth guard? Do they have a hard, low-cup chin strap? Is the chin strap fastened properly? The single most important thing a medical professional can do is make sure that they don't rush the athlete back on the field after sustaining a concussion.

16. *When you look at the marks on a helmet postgame, where should you see the marks?*

You do not want to see any marks on the top of the helmet's shell. You want to make sure that the athletes have their heads up. Any time you see deep gouges in the helmet, you need to talk to that player about how they are using the helmet, because that means that they are using the helmet more as a tool to hit another player rather than a protective device to keep their head safe.

17. *Should children wear helmets when riding their bikes in the neighborhood?*

   You want to keep the impact from going to the head, and a helmet is the best way to do that. So children should definitely be wearing helmets when riding a bicycle, motorcycle, four-wheeler, skateboard, etc.

18. *What is the purpose of the face mask?*

   When I was growing up, I was told that the face mask was put on the helmet to protect the face, to keep the elbows away from the nose, to keep the teeth from getting knocked out, to keep jaws from getting punched, or getting hit in the mouth. Now they are trying to design the face mask to be integrated into the helmet to strengthen the helmet. Helmets flex, and, obviously, the front of the helmet is where it is most open and probably the weakest, so there are designers trying to engineer the face mask to strengthen the shell while protecting your face and teeth.

19. *What is the importance of the chin strap and what chin strap is most protective?*

   The most protective chin strap is a hard-cup chin strap, because you want something like a helmet that can absorb the energy from the impact, protect your jaw, and protect your chin from blows. I feel a deeper chin strap is better. These kids put these covers inside the chin strap, which fills the cup, and this obscures the chin from sitting down inside the cup and decreases the protection. The importance of the chin strap is that it assists or prevents the helmet from moving, and it is a critical piece of equipment which is very, very overlooked. If a player can take his helmet off without adjusting the chin strap, it is not fitted properly. The main items regarding a chin strap are to get a deep, hard-cup chin strap and learn how to properly fasten it.

20. *Do you have any other suggestions concerning fitting of equipment that you feel is important in decreasing the incidence of head/neck trauma in athletic competition?*

Make sure that you work with someone reputable to recondition your helmets, and get the helmets off of the field within five years. You need to rotate the helmets. If a team has fifty players, they need to buy ten to eleven helmets/year to accomplish this task. You need to have the helmets professionally fit, and you need to maintain the helmet. The athlete needs to be educated on the importance of the mouth guard, the chin strap, the proper fit, and to notify the equipment manager or coach if something is not right. I think those things will add to the safety of the football program.

CHAPTER 7

THE ROLE OF LEGISLATION IN PREVENTION OF CONCUSSION AND CHRONIC TRAUMATIC ENCEPHALOPATHY

In the NFL, getting a concussion is easy, but getting back on the field is more difficult, as stricter policies on concussion evaluation and return to play are developed. States, including Washington—the first in 2009—Oklahoma, and Massachusetts enacted legislation establishing rules for prevention, on-field diagnoses, and return-to-play guidelines involving sports-related concussions. The NFL commissioner sent letters to forty-four governors, urging them to adopt a version of the Zachary Lystedt Law, named for the Washington state middle-schooler left in a wheelchair from a second-impact concussion. In April 2009, the NCAA urged its members to mandate return-to-play policies. In the fall of 2010, the National Federation of High School Associations also introduced a new rule: "Any athlete who exhibits signs, symptoms or behaviors consistent with a concussion shall immediately be removed from the contest and shall not return to play until cleared by an appropriate health care professional" (Finder).

The determinate of who qualifies as an appropriate health-care professional, the length of time required before a return to play can be approved, and the method of verification for return to play will be left to the school districts, subject to controlling state law and rules by individual state associations. The following management protocol is based on current research and expert opinion, and is included in the appendix of the 2010–2011 NFHS rule book:

1. No athlete should return to play or practice on the same day of a concussion.

2. Any athlete suspected of having a concussion should be evaluated that day.

3. Any athlete suspected of having a concussion should be medically cleared by an appropriate health-care professional prior to resuming participation in any practice or competition.

4. After medical clearance, return to play should follow a step-wise protocol with provisions for delayed return to play based upon the return of any signs or symptoms.

In October 2009 and January 2010, the House Judiciary Committee held two hearings about football brain injuries. Representative Linda T. Sanchez played a video interview with Dr. Ira Casson. He was the co-chairman of the NFL's concussion committee. In the video, Dr. Casson denied the health risks of concussions. Representative Sanchez said, "It sort of reminds me of the tobacco industry companies pre-1990s, when they kept saying no, there is no risk between smoking and damage to your health." After the 2009 hearing, the players' union did not think Dr. Casson was the right person to lead the NFL research study, as he often disagreed with research linking concussions and long-term results. Dr. Casson and his co-chair resigned in November 2010.

The House Committee grappling with the answers as to how to keep these young athletes safe heard testimonies from an NFL player who recently retired because of post concussion problems, a mother whose son incurred brain damage while playing football for the University of Pennsylvania and committed suicide, and a high school girl unable to keep up with her classes after suffering a concussion on the soccer field.

Education and Labor Committee chairman George Miller cited estimates of three hundred thousand sports-related concussions a year. Miller has introduced legislation that would require school districts to develop plans for concussion safety and management, and increases student and parent awareness of their dangers. Schools would also be required to provide support for students recovering from concussions (Abrams).

Congressional interest in legislation to protect young athletes from concussion has been so popular that one House committee held a hearing on one concussion bill, while another committee passed a different bill on concussion just four hundred feet down the hall.

In October 2010, Dr. Julian Bailes, who, in my opinion, is one of the top experts in the nation on brain research, testified on the impact of head injuries in the NFL. Afterward, John Conyers of the House Judiciary Committee said that the group will, "look into what can be done to limit head injuries in the NFL and compensate players and their families."

Conyers's announcement of the hearing was soon after the University of Michigan's Institute for Social Research released its findings from a study of retired NFL players. The study showed that retired NFL players aged thirty to forty-nine are nineteen times more likely to have been diagnosed with dementia, Alzheimer's, or other memory-related diseases than the general US male population. The list of witnesses asked to testify at the hearing included NFL commissioner Roger Goodell, former Pittsburgh Steeler Merril Hoge, former New York Giant Tiki Barber, and Steelers team physician Dr. Joseph Maroon.

Julian Bailes was one of the five neurosurgeons who testified. Dr. Bailes has studied the effects of concussion in football in 2000, when he set up the Center for the Study of Retired Athletes at the University of North Carolina–Chapel Hill. Dr. Bailes has studied the brains of numerous deceased athletes found to have suffered from chronic traumatic encephalopathy. Dr. Bailes and his colleague, Kevin Guskiewicz, have written clinical studies that link concussions and traumatic head injury to increased rates of mental illness in retired professional football players. Dr. Bailes made the comment that the NFL should change the rules for lineman. He said he would also stop all head contact in football practices (Albergotti and Wang).

The old NFL standard, established in 2007, stated an athlete should not be allowed to return to play on the same day if he lost consciousness. The new policy states: "Once removed for the duration of a practice or game, the player should not be considered for return-to-football activities until he is fully asymptomatic, both at rest and after exertion, has a normal neurological exam, normal neuropsychological testing, and has been cleared to return by both his team physician(s) and the independent neurological consultant" (Fendrich).

Chapter 8

Matt's Story: A Football Player Who Collapsed After a Football Game and Died of a Brain Hemorrhage, Written by His Mother/MJ's Story: A Fifteen-Year-Old Who Had a Bicycle Wreck Without a Helmet and Sustained a Life-Threatening Head Trauma/Skull Fracture, Written by His Father/Other Case Studies of Athletes Who Suffered Concussion and/or Neck Trauma

Matthew Ault's Story: Written by His Mother

Matthew Blair Ault, seventeen, was a three-sport athlete at Meigs High School. As a junior, he was a member of the 1996 baseball team that reached the Ohio High School Athletic Association Division III State Baseball Championship game. He also wrestled for three years and was a starting defensive back for the 1996 Marauder football team his senior year.

On October 18, 1996, Matthew collapsed outside the locker room after a 21–20, come from behind win over the Waverly Tigers. He was transported to a local hospital in the Waverly area and then flown to The Ohio State University Trauma Center, where he died on October 19.

An autopsy was conducted, and it was determined Matthew's death was the result of swelling of the brain caused by a brain hemorrhage. The autopsy report stated, "It is possible that the hemorrhage was caused by a direct blow to the head   it's possible that this injury was sustained while playing football."

The days leading up to the game, Matthew didn't show any major signs that something might be wrong. He complained of a slight headache a few days before the game and of a stiff neck the morning of the game, but nothing after that. At half-time of the game, he asked one of the coaches for some aspirin for his headache, which was not given to him. He denied any prior injury or any other symptoms of concussion. He stated he had sinus headaches. His exam was normal, and he was laughing and joking. He stated his headache had completely subsided before leaving the locker room at half time.. He finished the remainder of the game without any further complaints. He even celebrated the win with his teammates after the game, but as he took off his helmet and walked off the field to the locker room, he told a coach that the lights were, "killing my head." He collapsed and never regained consciousness.

Looking back, it's quite possible Matthew sustained the initial injury days or weeks before the night he collapsed. The game the week before was very physical, and Matthew took and delivered some hard hits. On October 18, everything cumulated in the tragic outcome.

Since then, everyone affected by Matthew's death has learned a great deal about head injuries, the signs and symptoms, and the devastating results that can be caused by repetitive blows to the head.

Matthew's family and friends encourage everyone to become familiar with the signs and symptoms of head injuries and to take every precaution when a head injury is suspected.

Matthew is sadly missed by all who knew and loved him.

MJ's Story: Written by His Father

On 6/14/05, our lives were changed in just a matter of seconds. Our son was a fifteen-year-old, 6'1", 220-pound teenager, way too big to wear a helmet. Or so he thought.

About 7 p.m. on 6/14/05, the father of one of my son's friends knocked on the door and said, "MJ wrecked his bicycle. I think he lost a tooth, and he is in the ER." We went to the ER, asked for MJ's room, and were told we would have to wait, as they were intubating him. That's when we knew it was more than just a lost tooth. The doctor came over to us and said, "You need to tell him that you love him, because he may not make it." We went in to see him and lost it. It did not even look like our son lying there, with all the blood, his eyes were bulged out, his nose was stuffed with gauze dripping with blood, and he had a tube in his throat helping him breathe.

They took MJ to Children's Hospital in Columbus, Ohio by Life Flight. It was an agonizing ninety-minute drive, not knowing whether he would live. He had an epidural hematoma, subdural hematoma, sinus fractures, basic skull fractures, and a left radius fracture. They told us the next seventy-two hours were critical, and if he survived until then, there would be a chance he would live. But they could not tell us what quality of life he might have. MJ was in a coma for about eight days. After he regained consciousness, we watched our son try to feed himself. He had to relearn how to write his name, dress himself, and walk again. It has been a long drawn-out recovery, but we realize we are fortunate he even survived.

Please know that, as a parent, you have to be the tough guy sometimes and enforce safety rules, such as making your child wear a helmet when riding a bicycle, scooter, rollerblades, four-wheeler, motorcycle, and so on. Don't worry about how "uncool" it may be to wear a helmet or think, *Well, my friends and I rode bikes and jumped ramps all my life, and nothing bad ever happened to us.* It only takes a small rock in the road or a crack in the pavement: one little incident. Step up and make the right choice to save your child's life! You won't regret it.

Parents of MJ Russell

Other Case Studies

1. *Rose Football Player Died of Second-Impact Syndrome*

   A junior running back left the field after being tackled in a football game and collapsed on the sideline. He was taken to the hospital, where he was placed on life support. He died the next day. This athlete reportedly has been hit in practice two days before the game and suffered a mild concussion. The cause of death was thought to be from a, "very rare condition which can occur when two relatively minor head injuries occur in a short time interval. It usually occurs in young athletes and is very rapidly fatal" (Candon).

2. A Spring Hill High School senior died a day after collapsing on the sideline at a football game.

   This athlete's parents had little reason to doubt that their seventeen-year-old son was ready to return to football. After sustaining a concussion in the homecoming game, he spent weeks resting, his CT scan was normal, and his medical doctor cleared him to play. The coroner determined, "The running back and linebacker died of a rare but severe brain injury which likely occurred during the earlier game which was undetected" ("Football Player's").

3. A sixteen-year-old football player developed a headache following a collision during a game.

   After a week of persistent headaches, a CT of the brain was performed and found to be negative, and a concussion was diagnosed. The athlete reported disappearance of all symptomology after seventeen days. Further testing failed to re-create symptoms. The athlete continued to deny any symptoms and was cleared to return to play thirty days after the initial injury. In the next game, "The athlete collided with an opposing player, ran to the sidelines and deteriorated on the sidelines after complaining of dizziness." EMS intubated him, and he was transported the ER. He was diagnosed with a right subdural hematoma by attending neurosurgeons. A burr hole craniotomy evacuated the lesion. The operative report noted a second area of chronic membrane formation consistent with past head trauma. This lesion had been undetected on two previous CT scans. In an interview four months later, the athlete admitted, "having experienced constant symptoms between the first and second injuries" (Litt).

4. An eighteen-year-old football player, with an unremarkable medical history, was walking toward the sideline and appeared confused as he took off his helmet. He fell to his knees and began to vomit.

   His immediate complaints were severe head pain, nausea, and vertigo. He denied neck pain or any lower or upper extremity numbness or tingling, and he was oriented to person, place, and time. The athlete admitted he had taken two hard hits during the game, which he recalled, and that he had a headache and nausea, which he did not report to the coaches or athletic trainer. The athlete was transported to the ER to prevent a possible catastrophic injury. While the athlete was being placed in the squad, his level of consciousness decreased, and he appeared to have a mild seizure, becoming unresponsive to stimuli. He was incontinent of urine. Intubation attempts were unsuccessful due to his resistance. CT revealed a left, frontal-temporal, acute, subdural hematoma, which did not end up requiring surgical intervention. The athlete recovered within a month. He was restricted from all physical activity until fully asymptomatic and cleared by the physician, and was restricted from contact sports for at least one year to be reevaluated at the end of that year (Logan, Bell, and Leonard).

5. An eighteen-year-old high school football player developed symptoms of decreased sensation and muscle weakness of the right leg during a time-out.

   He was removed from play for sideline evaluation. On initial presentation, he was alert with no other complaints. The athlete denied any specific impacts. During the initial exam, the athlete complained of immediate intense right temporal headache. Within one to two minutes, new symptoms of nausea, vomiting, convulsions, and a rapid loss of consciousness were demonstrated. The athlete was transported via air flight to a level one trauma center. A CT scan demonstrated a large, right-side subdural hematoma. The hematoma was surgically excised, revealing two lesions: one old and one acute. The athlete's parents revealed that three days prior to this event, after a football practice, the athlete had complained of headache, fatigue, and listlessness.

6. A fourteen-year-old girl sustains concussion from whiplash injury while doing repetitive back flips on a trampoline with a teenage friend, unsupervised by staff.

   On the way home, she informed her friend's mom that she had a bad headache. The mom gave her Tylenol and instructed the young girl to lie down and rest. The young girl went to sleep at the friend's house. The other teens woke her up to go swimming about an hour later. She already had her bathing suit on and states that she stood in the pool, dazed.

She remembers she couldn't say what she was trying to say: her words were jumbled. The girls thought their friend was acting unusual but thought she was just upset, because her mom would not let her go to the football game with them that night. They left her in the water and went to the pool house to get drinks. The young girl knew something was wrong, got out of the pool, and went upstairs to get dressed. When the other girls came up to get dressed, they found the teenage girl standing there with her shorts on as a top. She was confused and disoriented. The girls called the girl's mom, and the friend's mom took her to the ER. By the time they arrived at the ER, the young teen did not know anyone. And although she was typically a quiet, shy girl, she became combative in the ER when the nurse tried to cath her. A CT was taken of her head, and she was diagnosed with a Grade II concussion and sent to a level-one trauma center an hour away. She was taken out of athletics for three weeks and returned without any further problems. It was determined that the repetitive flips may have caused a whiplash injury, causing the concussion.

These case studies emphasize the importance of educating the athletes to be honest about their symptoms and to report them immediately. They also point out how important it is to educate parents and the public about how to identify the signs/symptoms of traumatic brain injury.

CHAPTER 9

THE LONG-TERM EFFECTS OF REPETITIVE HEAD TRAUMA/CHRONIC TRAUMATIC ENCEPHALOPATHY

Recent research has shown repetitive concussions can have long-term or permanent repercussions. Some believe the total effect of multiple blows to the head, even those that may not cause the athlete to have symptoms, can be more significant than sustaining one severe concussion with loss of consciousness.

Doctors Julian Bailes and Bennet Omalu revealed extensive brain damage when they examined Chris Henry's brain. Chris Henry played in only fifty-five NFL games, never missing one because of a concussion. The troubled receiver for the Cincinnati Bengals was arrested five times and served three suspensions, totaling fourteen games. He died after supposedly leaping from the back of a moving pickup after reportedly telling his fiancée, "If you take off, I'm going to jump from the truck and kill myself" (Finder, "Experts"). The brain of the late Cincinnati Bengals receiver contained many signs of chronic disease—sludge, tangles, and threads associated with late-in-life dementia or Alzheimer's disease—which may indicate it is possible that a football player can sustain life-altering head trauma without ever being diagnosed with a concussion. Dr. Bailes and Dr. Omalu, with the Brain Research Institute in Morgantown, West Virginia, have examined over ten other retired players, among them ex-Steelers Mike Webster, who was one of the first professional football players to be diagnosed with chronic traumatic encephalopathy (CTE).

Hall of Fame tight end John Mackey developed early-onset dementia. Andre Waters, a former NFL safety, killed himself in 2006, and researchers commented his brain looked like that of an eighty-five-year-old man. (Abel)

What Is CTE?

CTE is a degenerative brain disease that results in abnormal behaviors similar to those seen in individuals with Alzheimer's disease. Yet, unlike Alzheimer's, CTE has a clear environmental cause (repetitive brain trauma) rather than a genetic factor, making it the only preventable form of dementia (Ziegler). A number of neurological and physiological changes in the brain, including the accumulation of an abnormal protein called tau, is found in athletes with CTE. Symptoms of CTE include confusion; disorientation; dizziness; headache; lack of insight; poor judgment; staggered gait; impeded speech; tremors; vertigo; deafness; headaches; deterioration in attention, concentration, and memory; and dementia. The athlete may progress through many stages, including the initiation of affective disturbances and psychotic symptoms, with progression to social instability, erratic behavior, memory loss, and the initial onset of Parkinson's disease (McKee, Cantu, et al). The final stage consists of a progressive deterioration to dementia, and individuals often show signs of Parkinson's disease, gait abnormalities, speech difficulties, swallowing problems, and eyelid drooping.

How Is CTE Diagnosed?

CTE is diagnosed by studying brain tissue under a microscope. Although research has developed rapidly on this topic, no specific marker or test has been shown to detect CTE in a living athlete.

CTE was initially found in the brains of professional boxers, but researchers are now finding CTE in a number of athletes competing in various sports. According to McKee and associates (2009), of the fifty-one confirmed CTE cases, 90 percent occurred in athletes, including thirty-nine amateur and professional boxers, five football players, one professional wrestler, and one soccer player.

What Can Be Done to Prevent CTE?

We must focus on proper diagnosis and adhere to strict return-to-play guidelines. According to a statement in 2010 by Dr. Robert Stern , co-director of CSTE, new evidence shows, "85% of concussions require about three weeks of recovery" (Abel).

CTE appears to have the following sequence of events. Head trauma occurs. This leads to inflammation in the brain. This is followed by degeneration of brain tissue. This leads to an accumulation of tau protein and TDP-43. Then, the appearance of CTE occurs. The person's mental state deteriorates, depression sets in, and eventually, the athlete may become suicidal (Keaton).

Is There Any Treatment for CTE?

When swelling occurs from an injury, the first step is to put ice on the injury to reduce the inflammation. When head/neck trauma has occurred, ice can be placed on the back of the neck or on the head to reduce swelling. The next stage of prevention is to prevent brain degeneration. Cayce Health Database has suggested the use of gold chloride solution or gold sodium solution, as it is suggested to release electricity into the nervous system and reverse brain damage (Keaton).

The use of electric current in the brain is also being explored as a treatment option. This deep-brain stimulation is currently used to treat depression and epilepsy. Other suggested steps in treatment of CTE include consuming an alkaline diet; consuming adequate water, such as eight cups/day; and having an adequate intake of vitamins and minerals. Colon cleansing to eliminate toxins in the body has also been suggested as a possible treatment. Chiropractic care is suggested in order to make sure there is no spinal misalignment and that the neck curve is optimal (Keaton).

Alzheimer's & Dementia: The Journal of the Alzheimer's Association published a large, randomized, placebo-controlled nutritional study ("Brain Armor") that demonstrated the benefits of algal DHA in maintaining and improving brain health in older adults. In this study, healthy older adults (over age fifty-five) with a mild memory complaint who took 900mg algal DHA experienced significant reduction in errors on a memory test, compared to the performance of typical adults their age. The cognitive improvement demonstrated by the DHA supplemental group was equivalent to having the learning and memory skills of someone more than three years younger. Several products are now available with algal DHA, including Brain Armor, which is certified through NSF International's Certified for

Sport program, which screens for banned substances. Dr. Julian Bailes states, "Algal DHA supports brain and cardiovascular health. Brain Armor is a nutritional supplement that athletes should make a regular part of their health and welfare" ("Brain Armor").

Chapter 10

Common Questions Asked About Head/Neck Trauma and an Interview with Dr. Bill Moreau, US Olympic Committee Director of Sports Medicine Clinics

Question from a soccer mom:

"At what age is it safe to head the ball in soccer?"

"No child under the age of fourteen should head the ball," cautions Dr. Lyle Michell, chairman of the Sports Medicine Deptartment at Children's Hospital in Boston. He argues that kids have not fully developed the musculoskeletal maturity or coordination to handle a header properly until they're about fourteen years old ("The Human Brain").

Question from a dad whose ten-year-old wrecked his bike and hit his head on the pavement, sustaining a concussion:

"What caused my son's concussion when he hit his head?"

Within the skull, his gelatinous brain floats in a sea of cerebrospinal fluid that bathes and supports the brain, while acting as a shock absorber during rapid head movements. The outer surface of the head is smooth, but parts of the brain and inside the brain's surface are rough and jagged and can cause significant damage with acceleration/deceleration, creating a closed head injury. The brain rebounds back and forth against the skull's bony structures, causing damage to the brain ("The Human Brain").

Children suffer fifty thousand bicycle-related brain injuries in the United States each year, and more than four hundred die as a result. Wearing a helmet can reduce the severity of brain injury by as much as 85 percent ("The Human Brain"). However, half of all bike riders still do not wear a helmet.

Question from a wrestler's dad:

"My son's trainer told us to come and see you, because he thinks my son has a concussion. He had a bad headache after getting hit in the jaw at his wrestling match, and he was dizzy for about five minutes afterward but didn't pass out. How could he get a concussion from getting hit in the jaw?"

Concussion is not simply caused by a direct blow to the head. Blows to the face and jaw, which result in a force being transmitted to the brain, are also common causes of concussion (Kissick). A jolt to the head, jaw, head, face, neck, or chest can cause the brain to shift, causing a concussion. Another important concept to learn is that most concussions occur without loss of consciousness.

Question from a football player's mom:

"If the MRI or CT scan is normal, does that mean my son didn't have a concussion?"

No. Scans do not reveal whether a concussion has occurred. The scans are helpful in detecting life-threatening brain injuries, such as skull fractures, bleeding, or swelling of the brain. The diagnosis of a concussion is based on the history of how the injury occurred, observed signs and symptoms, and the physical exam, including cognitive testing, memory recall, balance testing, cranial nerve testing, neuromuscular testing, and vision testing by a properly trained sports practitioner.

Question from a wrestler's mother:

"How many concussions can an athlete have before he or she should stop playing sports?"

There is no "set number" of concussions that determine when an athlete should give up playing contact or collision sports. The circumstances surrounding each individual injury, presence of any cognitive defects, length of symptoms, history of past trauma, and how long it took to recover from those injuries must be considered. Athletes who are not fully recovered from an initial concussion are significantly vulnerable for recurrent, cumulative, and life-threatening conditions, such as second-impact syndrome.

Interview with Dr. Bill Moreau: US Olympic Committee Director of Sports Medicine Clinics

1. *As a sports chiropractic physician, what do you feel is the most important aspect in prevention of head/neck trauma in athletics (education, equipment, stricter rules, for example)?*

The old adage that an ounce of prevention is worth a pound of cure stands tall when it comes to the prevention of head and neck trauma in sports. Preventing head and neck trauma injuries in sports involves numerous factors for consideration. Sports-related head and neck trauma may or may not be prevented. There is always a risk of head and neck trauma when any individual participates in any activity. The multitude of variables to consider regarding preventing head and neck trauma are multifaceted and range from the mismatch of athletes, improper player technique, inadequate pre-participation examination, poor planning, and improper clearance to play after prior injury. To understand the range of the possible variables, the clinician first needs to develop an in-depth understanding of the possible etiologies of head and neck trauma in the specific sport they are covering.

Each sporting activity has unique peculiarities of injury patterns, technique, and equipment-related factors. All health-care providers covering sports are obligated to take the time to prepare to cover a sport by learning all they can about that sport. Some sports, such as synchronized swimming or Paralympic sled hockey, may not have substantial information available in the scientific literature to assist the clinician in these preparations. In these cases, the clinician first needs to identify their own sources of information. This self-directed research could include reading the rules, speaking with athletes and coaching staff, and most important, finding someone who has covered the event before to act as a mentor.

Some universal precautions and best practices are readily available. This type of information can universally apply to the management of head and neck trauma in all athletic situations. Some examples include the prehospital care of the spine-injured athlete or consensus statements. The best practices include clinical cornerstones, such as not returning a head-injured athlete to play before they are fully recovered, or treating all unconscious athletes as if they have a spinal injury. The clinician must prepare by accepting the challenge to be prepared for the unexpected. Diligent work is required to develop an in-depth understanding of what should be expected or what may randomly occur during an athletic event.

2. You cared for a football player with a serious head injury. Can you describe what happened?

Most clinicians cover sports because they love the game and the athletes who play it. Sports medicine providers are privileged to perform a small role in helping others to achieve their sports-related goals. Each health-care provider in sports medicine has a genuine interest not only in the overall field of sports medicine but also in specific areas of interest. For me, concussion has always been an area that stimulated my thinking. The primary reason concussion was, and still is, so important to me is that after all these years, the knowledge of concussion is still in transition. Concussion is a very common occurrence in sport, and if a clinician makes error in the evaluation or management of the concussed athlete, the result can be devastating.

This case concerns a high school football player. It was a great football Friday night in northwest Iowa, and all seemed right in the world, until an event occurred. After working the sidelines of many sports for over twenty-five years, the events from over a decade ago are still clearly resonating in my memory.

Most sports medicine providers use time-outs to perform a rapid check-in with the players. Late in the fourth quarter, the wide receiver from the sideline I was covering was observed to be leaning over with his hands on his thighs, as he stood just off to the side of the time-out huddle. This was odd, because the game was almost over, and it was an extremely close and challenging event. The player was also very well known to me as an ardent competitor. Why wasn't he engaging with the coach's instructions?

When I approached him and asked what was going on, he simply stated, "I can't feel my legs." A course of questioning was immediately pursued regarding any history of head, neck, or spinal trauma, which he denied. Even though he was pain free, alert, and oriented, it was obvious that he was not going to be allowed to continue playing until the etiology of the lack of sensation in his legs was identified. He was moved to the sideline for further evaluation. Cervical spine and cranial nerve evaluations were unremarkable. He had no complaints of pain or headache. Another physician joined me in evaluating the athlete. As the evaluation progressed, the athlete suddenly complained of an intense, sudden onset of right temporal headache. Within just a few minutes, he rapidly lost consciousness, displayed major motor seizure, demonstrated decorticate posturing, had no response to painful stimuli, and obvious unequal pupil size. The athlete's Glascow Coma Scale (GCS) was now a 3, when fewer than five minutes before, he demonstrated a normal GCS.

Oxygen was supplied through a non-rebreather mask (it was the first Friday night that oxygen was readily available on the sideline in the history of the school), and EMS was activated. The athlete was rapidly transferred via air ambulance one hundred miles to the closest hospital with a neurosurgeon on staff.

The first images from the head CT scan demonstrated a left midline shift of the brain, with collapse of the right ventricle secondary to a massive right acute subdural hematoma (ASDH) that extended from the frontal region to the occiput.

Emergency decompression surgery was performed with an amazingly positive result. Only a few months later, the athlete was back in school.

The important message here is about the importance of understanding that in sports medicine, especially as it applies to acute head and neck trauma, a cornerstone to care includes the required ability of the clinician to perform rapid analysis of an ever-changing diagnostic picture, resulting in the correct management decisions. ASDH is an uncommon occurrence in sport. The outcome for the athlete who suffers this type of brain injury will depend on many dynamics that range from controlled factors, such as the available equipment and care provided at the time of injury, to uncontrollable factors, such as the weather conditions related to the availability of rapid air transfer and the amount of brain damage that has already occurred from the bleeding and pressure on the brain.

Severe head and neck trauma will continue to occur in sport. There are many skills needed to manage the injured athlete. This case study presents the opportunity to reinforce a few clinical pearls that we all can carry forward.

1. Dedicated preparation from the sideline sports medicine staff is the key to providing individuals who have been seriously injured with head and neck trauma the opportunity to successfully recover.

2. The emergency care equipment that is readily available at an event will dictate the level of support that can be provided to the injured athlete.

3. An injured individual's health status can rapidly change. Serial (repeated) examinations should be performed every five minutes until the athlete's presentation is static.

4. Sports medicine can be an enjoyable endeavor, but sports coverage is not a good place for unsupervised on-the-job training. Success in sports medicine requires constant and in-depth preparation and understanding of head and neck trauma from the entire sports medicine team.

3. *In an abstract you wrote for the Sport Science Symposium, you concluded that forty-seven out of seventy-two athletes sustained symptoms consistent with concussion but did not report they had a problem (an estimated 65 percent of unreported concussions). What do you think can be done to get these athletes to admit they have symptoms to health-care staff and/or coach?*

> Sports-related concussion is the most commonly underreported serious injury in athletics. The actual number of concussions that actually occur in sporting activities is actually unknown. There are many reasons that athletes, who are much more aware that concussion requires an immediate medical assessment, do not report their injury to a health-care provider. It is my observation that almost all the reasons that cause athletes to hide their injury are based in the culture of athletics. This study, which investigated high school football, revealed that by far and away, the concussed athletes most commonly reported their injury to their teammates, not to the health-care providers, who were readily available on the sideline.

> All members of society must become engaged to change the athlete's perception of concussion. This includes coaches, parents, officials, sports medicine staff, media, rule makers, and the athletes themselves. Only by a consistent and concerted effort will we be able to get to ground zero, where together we can positively influence the athletes themselves.

4. *As the US Olympic Committee Director of Sports Medicine Clinics, have you experienced any unique cases of athletes with head/neck trauma? If so, please describe.*

> While I have been at the USOC, I would hesitate to say that we have seen unique head or neck trauma. We do evaluate, diagnose, and manage head trauma on a routine basis. Perhaps the uniqueness would be to the athletic population we serve.

> At the United States Olympic Committee's Training centers, we serve a very diverse, elite athletic populationThe athletes are of various ages and from different cultural backgrounds

and there is a wide range in skill level. There are over forty-five different sporting national governing bodies (NGBs) we work with. The many NGBs represent uniquely different sporting activities. For instance, US Ski and Snowboard represents ski jumping, downhill, snowboarding, acrobatic, moguls, and more! Then, you need to consider the Olympic and Paralympic branches of each sport. Some sports have a recognized higher frequency of head and spine injury, but virtually all sporting activities have an associated risk of head and neck injury.

5. What medical professionals do you feel are qualified to make return-to-play decisions for athletes who have sustained a sports-related head/neck injury?

This is an area of great controversy in sports, specifically in regards to managing the concussed athlete. In my personal opinion, there are many people who are qualified to make return-to-play decisions in sport. The easiest way to sort them is by their educational degree. The problem with this approach is that the degree does not necessarily define the individual competency in a very specific area of knowledge. There are many variables that will define if an individual is qualified to make return-to-play decisions. The first area to consider is the scope of practice. The law determines scope of practice, which, in turn, identifies if an action is lawful or not. Clearly, if an action is not lawful, it should not be done. Even if the scope of practice allows for an individual to take action, it is still the individual health-care provider who must be prepared to make the correct return-to-play decision. This preparation will not happen by accident. It will require a consistent and diligent effort by each health-care provider to keep informed regarding standards of care and examination skills. I have a saying that goes, "In sports medicine you need to know, what you need to know, before you need to know it!" In other words, sports medicine is not a kind or forgiving area for a "learn as you go it alone" approach to health care.

CONCLUSION

I wrote this book to educate the public about concussion and neck trauma. The potential severity of concussion can no longer be ignored. The risks are inherent in contact sports. Many, if not most, young boys dream of becoming football players. Football, like other sports, can teach young players many things. It can teach someone how to be a team player, how to work hard to accomplish a goal, and how to listen to those in authority. I am often asked if I feel a parent should allow his or her child to play contact sports. My answer is simple. Participation in contact sports is dangerous but no more dangerous than driving your car to take your child to school. If you don't follow the rules, don't pay attention to the road signs, drive while under the influence of alcohol, drive at excessive speeds, or drive a car that hasn't been maintained, your likelihood of being injured is drastically increased. You need to make sure all athletes follow the rules and learn and practice proper technique. They must be aware of the dangers of continuing to play with an injury, they must properly strengthen and condition their body for the sport, and they must properly wear and maintain their equipment.

Coaches, parents, and athletes should know that better equipment cannot entirely protect the head from concussion. Given the number of repetitive collisions in football, no helmet can entirely absorb the impact, and although medical research continues to make important contributions to better understand how and why athletes sustain concussions, there is still a lot we simply just don't know. For example, how many concussions cause a tendency to develop long-term effects on the brain? When is it safe to return to play after a concussion? What amount of impact is needed to cause a concussion?

The fact that well-intentioned physicians, trainers, researchers, and lawmakers have developed guidelines in concussion management is an important step, but guidelines are only as good as the quality of the evidence that supports them. Everyone must do their part in the prevention of head and neck trauma.

REFERENCES

Abel, D. "Bill Addressing Student Concussion Advances." *Boston Globe.* 28 April 2010. Web. Accessed 29 June 2010.

Abrams, Jim. "Lawmakers Seek to Protect Student Athletes' Heads." *Associated Press.* Sept. 2010. Web. Accessed 25 Sept. 2010. <http://www. google.hostednews/ap/article.

Albergotti, Reed, and Shirley S. Wang. "Is It Time to Retire the Football Helmet?" *Wall Street Journal Online.* 11 November 2009. Web. Accessed 1 Jan. 2011. <http://online.wsj.com/article/SB10001424052748704402404574527881984299454.html>.

Aubry, M., Cantu, R., Dvorak, J., et al. "Summary and Agreement Statement of the First International Conference on Concussion in Sport, Vienna, 2001: Recommendations for the improvement of safety and health of athletes who may suffer concussive injuries." *B.J. Sports Med.* 36 (2002):6–10. Print.

Bailes, Julian E., and Vincent Hudson. "Classification of Sport-Related Head Trauma: A Spectrum of Mild to Severe Injury." *Concussion in Athletes.* Spec. issue of *Journal of Athletic Training.* 36.3 (2001): 236–243. Print.

Bartrum, Michael. E-mail interview. 22 Jan. 2011.

"Brain Armor Can Help Maximize Athletic Performance." *Sports Dietitians. org.* Collegiate and Professional Sports Dietitians Association. n.d. Web. Accessed 9 Sept. 2011. <http://www.sportsdieticians.org/Brain_Armor. html>.

Brain-Pad: Protective Solutions. Brain-Pad°, Inc. n.d. Web. Accessed 17 Sept. 2011. <http://www.brainpads.com>.

Candon, Tim. "Rose football player died of Second Impact Syndrome." *Capitol Broadcasting Company.* 24. Sept. 2008. Web. Accessed 12 Nov. 2008. <http://www.highschoolot.com/content/story/3594964/?print_friendly=1>.

Cantu, Robert C. "Classification and Clinical Management of Concussion." *Neurological Sports Medicine: A Guide for Physicians and Athletic Trainers.* Julian E. Bailes and Arthur L. Day, eds. Rolling Meadows: American Association of Neurological Surgeons, 2001. 25–33. Print.

Cantu, Robert C. "Transient Quadraplegia: To Play or Not to Play." *Sports Medicine Digest.* 1994. Print.

"Concussion Facts." *Carolina Sports Concussion Program.* Carolina NeuroSurgery and Spine Associates, n.d. Web. Accessed 6 July 2009. <http://cnsa.com/concussion/facts.html.com>.

"Concussions." *About.com Orthopedics.* About.com, n.d. Web. Accessed 31 Oct. 2008. <http://orthopedics.about.com/od/sportsinjuries/a/concussion.htm>.

"Did You Know" *Traumatic Brain Injury.* University of Nebraska–Lincoln. n.d. Web. Accessed 6 July 2009. <http://tbi.unl.edu/savedTBI/sports/didyou.html>.

Duma, S. M., S. J. Manoogian, W. R. Bussone, et al. "Analysis of Real-Time Head Accelerations in Collegiate Football Players." *Clinical Journal of Sports Medicine.* 15:1 (2005): 3–8. Print.

Fendrich, Howard. "NFL Concussion Rule Changes: Stricter Guidelines Go Into Effect This Week." *Huff Post Sports.* The Huffington Post. 2 Dec. 2009. Web. Accessed 3 Feb. 2010. <http://www.huffingtonpost.com/2009/12/02/nfl-concussion-rule-chang_n_377907.html>.

Finder, Chuck. "Brain Injuries Penalize Football at All Levels." *Pittsburgh Post Gazette.* Post-Gazette.com. 19 Sept. 2010. Web. Accessed 25 Sept. 2010. <http://www.post-gazette.com/pg/10262/1088731-114.stm>.

Finder, Chuck. "Experts Warn About Repeated Brain Blows in Football."

Pittsburgh Post Gazette. Post-Gazette.com. 28 June 2010. Web. Accessed 25 Sept. 2010. <http://www.post-gazette.com/pg/10179/1068847-114.stm >.

"Football Player's Death Points to Screening Limits for Concussions." *Sports Illustrated.com.* 3 Dec. 2 010. Web. Accessed 1 Jan. 2011. <http://sportsillustrated.cnn.com/2010/highschool/12/03/fbh-player-death.ap/index.htm>.

Goldman, Tom. "Concussion Worries Renew Focus on Football Safety." NPR. 24 Sept. 2010. Web. Accessed 1 Jan. 2011. <http://www.npr.org/templates/story/story.php?storyId=130081779>.

Guskiewicz, K. M., J. P. Mihalik, V. Shankar, et al. "Measurement of Head Impacts in Collegiate Football Players: Relationship Between Head Impact Biomechanics and Acute Clinical Outcome After Concussion." *Neurosurgery.* 61:6 (2007): 1244–1252. Print.

Guskiewicz, K. M., S. L. Bruce, R. C. Cantu, et al. "National Athletic Trainers' Association Position Statement: Management of Sport-Related Concussion." *Journal of Athletic Training.* 39 (2004): 280–297. Print.

"The Human Brain—Watch Your Head." *Fi.edu.* The Franklin Institute. n.d. Web. Accessed 3 Feb. 2010. <http://www.fi.edu/learn/brain/head.html>.

Keaton, Elva. "How to Cure Chronic Traumatic Encephalopathy CTE—Cayce Approach." *Suite 101.com.* 3 July 2011. Web. Accessed 13 Sept. 2011. <http://www.suite101.com/content/how-to-cure-chronic-traumatic-encephalopathy-cte.com>.

Kissick, Jamie. "New Concussion Management Guidelines: Concussion Question and Answer Document for Physicians." *ThinkFirst-SportSmart Concussion Education and Awareness Program.* n.d. Web. Accessed 6 July 2009. <http://www.doctorsns.com/content/concussionguidelines_public.htm>.

Kleiner, D. M., J. L. Almquist, J. Bailes, P. Burruss, et al. *Prehospital Care of the Spine-Injured Athlete: A Document from the Inter-Association Task Force for Appropriate Care of the Spine-Injured Athlete.* Dallas, Texas. National Athletic Trainers' Association, March 2001. Print.

Litt, D. "Acute Subdural Hematoma in a High School Football Player." *Journal of Athletic Training. (2001):*69–71. Print.

Logan, S., G. Bell, and C. Leonard. "Acute Subdural Hematoma in a High School Football Player After 2 Unreported Episodes of Head Trauma: A Case Report." *Journal of Athletic Training.* (2001): 433–436. Print.

Maiese, Kenneth. "Introduction: Head Injuries." *Merck Manual Home Edition.* Jan. 2008. Web. Accessed 22 Feb. 2011. <http://www.merckmanuals.com/home/sec06/ch087/ch087a.html>.

"Manual A: Concussion Management & Sentinel Reports—A Guide for the People Who Care for America's Athletes." *Concussion Sentinel.* Release 3, Revision 1.0. n.d.

Mayfield: Your Total Neurosurgical Resource. Mayfield Clinic, 2009. Web. Accessed 7 July 2009. <http://www.mayfieldclinic.com>.

McKee, A. C., R. C. Cantu, C. J. Nowinski, E. T. Hedley-Whyte, B. E. Gavett, et al. "Chronic Traumatic Encephalopathy in Athletes: Progressive Taupathy After Repetitive Head

Injury." *Journal of Neuropathology and Experimental Neurology* 68:7 (2009): 709–735. Print.

McMaster University. "Mouthguards and Concussion Prevention." *Brain-Pad Blog.* 17 Sept. 2010. Web. Accessed 17 Sept. 2011. <http://blog.brainpads.com/?p=88>.

Mihalik, J. P., D. R. Bell, S. W. Marshall, and K.M. Guskiewicz. "Measurement of Head Impacts in Collegiate Football Players: An investigation of Positional and Event-type Differences." *Neurosurgery.* 61:6 (2007): 1229–1235. Print.

Moreau, Bill. E-mail interview. 9 March 2011.

National Operating Committee on Standards for Athletic Equipment. NOCSAE. n.d. Web. Accessed 3 Feb. 2010. <http://www.nocsae.org/about/history.htm>.

"New Football Helmet Detects Impacts That May Cause Traumatic Brain Injury: Neurophilosophy." 10 Sept. 2007.

Web. Accessed 9 Sept. 2010. <http://scienceblogs.com/ neurophilosophy/2007/09/_american_footbal_players_are.php?refer >.

"NFL Still Gathering Data on Concussions After Instituting a New Policy." Web. Accessed 25 Sept. 2010.

Ommaya, A. K., and T. A. Gennarelli. "Cerebral Concussion and Traumatic Unconcsciousness: Correlation of Experimental and Clinical Observations of Blunt Head Injuries." *Brain.* 97:4 (1974): 633–654. Print.

Peng, Ry, Y. B. Gao, Xy Xiao, et al. "Study on the Expressions of Basic Fibroblast Growth Factor and Nervous Growth Factor in Rat Cerebral Concussion." *Zhongguo Wei Zhong Bing Ji Jui Yi Xue.* 15 (2003): 213–216. Print.

"Physician Referral Checklist." *Journal of Athletic Training.* 39:3. Appendix B. Sept. 2004. Print.

Pociask, Frederick D. *Cranial Nerve Examination and Evaluation Study Guide.* Wayne State University Department Health Care Sciences. n.d. Web. Accessed 7 July 2009. <healthcaresciencescw.wayne.edu/cnm/start. htm>.

"Position Statement: The Prevention of Injuries in Amateur Football." Michigan Governor's Council on Physical Fitness, Health and Sports. n.d. Web. Accessed 3 Feb. 2010. <http://www.mdch.state.mi.us/pha/vipf2/ football.htm>.

"Preventing Severe Head and Neck Injuries in High School and Collegiate Athletes." *News Blaze.* NewsBlaze LLC. 1 Nov. 2005. Web. Accessed 7 July 2009. <http://newsblaze.com/story/2005/900002.www/topstory.htm>.

"Revolution Helmet: Research Findings." *Riddell Sports Group.* 2006. Print.

Robinson, R. G. "Chronic Subdural Hematoma: Surgical Management in 133 Patients." *Journal of Neurosurgery.* 61 (1984): 263–268. Print.

"School of Hard Knocks." *Brain-Pad Protective Solutions.* Brain-Pad Inc. n.d. Web. Accessed 25 March 2007.<http://www.brainpads.com/2006%20 graphics/20060921_101017_ConcussionFoot092206 >.

Starkey, Jonathan. "Head Games: Concerns About the Long-Term

Effects of Concussions Prompt Companies to Redesign Football Helmets." *Washington Post.* 10 Nov. 2009. Web. Accessed 1 Jan. 2011. <http://www.washingtonpost.com/wp-dyn/content/article/2009/11/06/AR2009110603465.html>.

Stein S. C., and S. E. Ross. "Mild Head Injuries: A Plea for Early CT." *Journal of Trauma.* 33 (1992): 11–13. Print.

"Traumatic Brain Injury." *Brain Injury Permanency from Concussion.* The Brain Injury Law Group. n.d. Web. Accessed 11 Oct. 2010. <http://www.subtlebraininjury.com>.

Ziegler, Terry. "Chronic Traumatic Encephalopathy." *SportsMD.com.* 14 Oct. 2010. Web. Accessed 13 Sept. 2010. <http://www.sportsmd.com/Articles/id/44/cid/1/n/chronic_traumatic-encephalopathy.aspx.com>.

ABOUT THE AUTHOR

Dr. Kelly Roush is a certified chiropractic sports physician, certified athletic trainer, and the director of Sports Medicine Services at a 140-physician Multidisciplinary Clinic. She has hospital privileges at two hospitals and has served as a team physician for the past sixteen years: thirteen years at Meigs High School (Ohio), three years at Point Pleasant High School (West Virginia), ten years at the University of Rio Grande, and she assists with sports injury coverage at two local gymnastic centers. She speaks both locally and nationally at conferences on the topic of concussion and neck trauma. She is driven and fervent when it comes to providing the best care possible for athletes. Dr. Roush has been instrumental in helping athletes with opportunities at the collegiate level and has assisted athletes with their quest to qualify for the Olympics. Dr. Roush has treated/ trained athletes at all levels, including Olympic athletes, NFL players, college athletes, pro baseball players, semipro hockey players, high school athletes, and younger kids. She is extremely passionate about sports as she played volleyball, basketball, and softball, and cheered in high school and received a full scholarship to play volleyball in college. Serving as a sports physician is much more than a career; it is where her heart lies. Dr. Roush loves spending time with her family and serving God. She loves providing health care for the athletes she serves, and the sports arena is her mission field.